Two Six Shooters
Beat Four Aces

TWO SIX SHOOTERS BEAT FOUR ACES
STORIES OF A YOUNG ARIZONA

BARBARA MARRIOTT

TWODOT®

GUILFORD, CONNECTICUT
HELENA, MONTANA

A · TWODOT® · BOOK

An imprint and registered trademark of Rowman & Littlefield

Distributed by NATIONAL BOOK NETWORK

Copyright © 2015 by Barbara Marriott

British Library Cataloguing-in-Publication Information available

Library of Congress Cataloging-in-Publication Data

Marriott, Barbara.
  Two six shooters beat four aces : stories of a young Arizona / Barbara Marriott.
    pages cm
  Includes bibliographical references and index.
  ISBN 978-1-4422-4731-4 (pbk.)—ISBN 978-1-4422-4732-1 (ebook) 1. Arizona—History—Anecdotes. 2. Arizona—Biography—Anecdotes. 3. Frontier and pioneer life—Arizona—Anecdotes. I. Title.
  F811.6.M37 2015
  979.1—dc23
                                    2015012471

∞™ The paper used in this publication meets the minimum requirements of American National Standard for Information Sciences—Permanence of Paper for Printed Library Materials, ANSI/NISO Z39.48-1992.

For Gene and Irwin Pellerin, John and Geri Redling, and Kathy and Tom Steckler, who fill the road of life with laughs and love.

Acknowledgments

No author writes alone. Behind him or her, there is an army of supporters, helpers, informants, well-wishers, and production people. That is especially true in nonfiction. First thanks go to Melanie Sturgeon from the Arizona State Library, Archives, and Public Records, who made the Federal Writers' Project papers available. Thank you God for Erin Turner, who is one of the fairest and best editors in the business, and thanks to my right-hand-man Mike, who supplies transportation, opinions, and the correct spelling. When encouragement is needed, when the writing path is gloomy or nonexistent, Jan Cleere, author and friend, always has the right words, the best advice, and the most cheerful smile. "Let's do lunch!" We do, and it lasts until dinnertime. Barbara Akins is my cheerful and efficient partner at book fairs. Her professional manner takes a lot of stress away from me, and I don't know how, but she manages to organize chaos. Oh, how I appreciate you. There are not enough thanks and appreciation I can lay on my family, Bill and Candy Marriott, Minette and Mike Shook, and the grand-adults: Tyler, Casey, and Matt and the newest additions, Katie and Brandon . . . they are always there for me.

Contents

Author's Preface

The world of men is best captured through the lives of the men who created history.

—Plutarch

During the American Depression of the 1930s, the very core of the American nation had eroded to a sad, unstable state. The unemployment rate was at 20 percent, a figure that did not include women workers. These dire circumstances brought about the creation of the Works Progress Administration (WPA) by the newly elected president, Franklin Delano Roosevelt. The WPA operated from 1934 until the demands of our involvement in World War II closed the last of the program in 1943.

Under the WPA umbrella, Roosevelt and his cabinet set about creating agencies and labor projects that would immediately put the American people back to work. However, the government knew it would take more than physical labor to help America recover. The mind and spirit of Americans required the same attention as the roads and buildings of our country. For while engineers, construction workers, farmers, and furniture makers needed jobs, so did musicians, actors, dancers, artists, and writers.

With the encouragement, and sometimes insistence, of Eleanor Roosevelt, the president's wife, the government established a series of federal agencies to aid these unemployed creative workers. Mrs. Roosevelt believed their products would lift up the broken spirit of Americans.

Starting in 1934, America underwent a monumental change. Newly constructed highways crisscrossed the countryside, bringing Americans physically closer together. Federal buildings graced our towns and cities and made doing business easier and more pleasant. Locally inspired dramas, dance, art, and music flourished and was accessible to all with inexpensive or free venues.

In 1935 the WPA created the Federal Writers' Project (FWP) as one of their programs. The main mission of the FWP was to collect information for individual state guidebooks. These books were not only for visiting foreigners, but also for Americans. The premise was that employment and good roads would encourage travel, and the guidebooks would introduce our country's heritage to all travelers, feature our unique natural attractions, and instill pride in Americans.

The guidebooks were to be more than facts, figures, and pictures of shrines and temples. They were to be about the regional people, and their culture. Washington wanted the books to portray not only history, but also lifestyles. Interviewers in the young state of Arizona gathered information, biographies, and historical data on their pioneers. They wove mini biographies into the contents of the guidebooks.

Ross Santee, artist, writer, and cowboy, headed up the Arizona Federal Writers' Project (FWP). Arizona interviewers collected information on 141 women and 137 men. Some of the pioneers were paid fifty cents to tell their story, which was the going rate for FWP interviews. Many volunteered their stories for nothing. They talked about themselves and the Arizona characters they knew.

In Our Own Words, published in 2009 is the verbatim interviews of the women pioneers. Women came because of their families. For the men it was a personal decision . . . men came because they chose to. Of course, some boys had no choice. Women shared stories about relationships and family hardships. Men told tales of adventure and daring deeds. Men spoke of grandiose plans, failures, and incredible danger, much of which they brought on themselves. Together the interviews give insight, from the grassroots level, of the building of a state's spirit and character.

The men interviewed were not all rich and famous; actually few were. They were mostly poor and ordinary. However, among them were distinguished men and a few despicable men, for they were a realistic representation of the male pioneer population during the territory's early days. The pioneers arrived to settle a territory rich in history, a history that started well before AD 900 with the ancient Native Americans, a history embolden by the conquering Conquistadores.

Because of their content, the men's interviews needed something more than the exact words of their trials in the West. Their stories needed a broader view of the Old West, and that created questions, such as: What attracted them to this vast wilderness? How did they chose to earn a living? What were their contributions, good and bad, to the history of Arizona?

The pioneer men's memories of events and characters cover a period from 1830 to 1923. During that time, the Arizona Territory grew from a population of 40,400 to over 204,354. Today her population exceeds 6,600,000.

By 1943, the WPA was no longer a priority for this country; we were at war and America's efforts, attention, and resources went toward the effort to win World War II. Sometime in the post–World War II years, the state of Arizona collected all of their Federal Writers' Project papers, files, and documents from the federal government and placed them in the state's various archival systems. For over seventy years the original interviews lay dormant, first in the archives of Washington, DC, then in Arizona, where they were scattered between Flagstaff and Phoenix.

In 2012, Arizona celebrated her one hundredth anniversary of statehood. What better way to celebrate than to look back at the information captured by the FWP, when the state was only in its twenties? A look at the files revealed a treasure trove of historical facts, fascinating oral histories, and information that portrayed the Old West as it really was—a wild, challenging, dangerous, and sometimes humorous world.

It took extraordinary men and women to settle a state and build a strong nation, and they came. For many the beauty attracted them. A beauty brazenly emphasized with bold colors, contrasting textures, and seductive promises. The land played to their greed, their sense of adventure, their wish for a different life. Arizona knew all the tricks. The adventuresome saw her innocence; the land's deceptive ways made them believe she could be easily conquered and tamed. However, Arizona had a wily side, one that could lead to cruelty and death as easily as riches and fame.

When Jose Castro and other FWP interviewers collected this information from and about Arizona pioneer men, they thought they were only doing a job for the federal government. In reality, what they did was capture a thick slice of Arizona history, not in dry data, but in the words of those who lived the pioneer life.

The speakers could have been out on the range, around a campfire swapping stories with the smoke and their tales drifting up, disappearing in the night sky. They could have been in a saloon, the air thick with the yeasty smell of beer and the smoky smell of whiskey, as the storyteller stared into the distance, leaned back, and spun his tale.

The reality was that the setting was none of these romantic places, but instead their own home, or the home of someone they hardly knew, or even a neutral place that belonged to no one. The venue didn't matter; it was all about their memories. They talked about the men they knew, the men they heard of, and their own lives when they were young, adventurous, and at times reckless.

Perhaps time had faded some memories, exaggerated others, and elaborately filled in the memory blanks. It didn't really matter, because reality is only what a person remembers, and people remember what is important to them. Everything these men said was important to them.

The listener scribbled notes, occasionally leaning forward to catch the words, and ask questions. What questions, we will never know because there were no records kept of interview questions and no standard procedure for the FWP interviewers to follow. Format wasn't important, content was the treasure.

The treasure the Arizona pioneer men delivered described the birth, spirit, and character of a state; so powerful were the accountings that they make Western fiction pale. The men who lived the life and now relived it in their memories spun the reality of the Old West.

The facts and descriptions here are from the interviews, and there are many direct quotes and timely expressions. This is a book of adventure and men's dreams, and because it is true, it is even more unbelievable than a work of fiction or fantasy.

Except for the Arizona history comments, the information and quotes in this book are from the interviews and biographies in the records of the Arizona Federal Writers' Project.

Introduction

*Alpine Valleys, scorching deserts, and broken mountain chains . . . ruled
by the most vindictive and warlike of all Redmen, the Apaches . . .*
                                        —CHARLES DEBRILLE POSTON

THE HISTORY AND POLITICS OF 1800 ARIZONA

In the early 1800s, the southwest lands had little appeal for most Americans.
In 1851, Charles Debrille Poston, considered by many to be the father of
Arizona, described the land as "having great rivers that over drained the
land." Poston noted that the diverse topography of "Alpine valleys, scorching
deserts, and broken mountain chains provide a varied climate." He added
that the land was "ruled by the most vindictive and warlike of all Redmen,
the Apaches, and there is no settlement east or west, between the Colorado
and the Rio Grande rivers." While colorful, and somewhat accurate, Poston's
statement totally ignored the small Mexican pueblos in the territory.

Although Poston thought little of the land, he did have the honor
of naming the territory. When the attorney general of New Mexico sent
a petition to Congress asking for separation of the government land
between Colorado and the Rio Grande Rivers (now Arizona and New
Mexico), Poston suggested the name "Arizona," from the Aztec word
Arisuma, meaning "rocky country."

There were a few white men living in the territory; most of them had
fled justice in other states or territories. However, they were soon to learn
that there was no sanctuary in the sparsely populated Mexican villages.
The Mexicans took out their frustrations with their government, and their
resentment of the United States, through lawlessness. As Poston put it, "It
was the reign of the revolver. You had to carry a knife and a gun for your
life. Men only lived if they were quicker on the draw."

This land came to the attention of the American public in 1836. An area of northern Mexico, called Texas, wanted independence and freedom from Mexican control. That year, after a series of skirmishes, the Texans finally gained their independence. It came at a cost of many lives, including the men lost in the devastating fight at an obscure mission, where the Texan rallying battle cry of "Remember the Alamo" was born.

Mexico did not give up the Texas land willingly. They continued to encourage border raids. Then, in a threat to the United States, they warned that any attempt at annexing Texas would lead to war.

American president James Polk saw the situation differently. He was on a political path of "manifest destiny," believing America had the right, almost the duty, to spread its boundaries from sea to sea. He saw the annexation of Texas as a step in that direction. The implied economic benefits of expanding the borders across the continent were enormous, especially after the discovery of gold in California.

Polk offered to purchase the coveted land from Mexico. When they refused, he moved troops into the zone between the Rio Grande and Nueces Rivers. There, on April 25, 1846, a troop of Mexican cavalry attacked the encamped soldiers, killing almost a dozen. The Mexican soldiers went on to mount another attack against an American fort on the Rio Grande. That was all the excuse Polk needed to pressure Congress into declaring war.

Meanwhile, long after the Conquistadors had come and gone, another religious movement was to play an important historic role in this southwest land. Unlike the Franciscan and Jesuit priests, from the 1500s and 1600s, this religious group was not looking to co-op those who lived on the land, nor did they seek to rape the land of its riches. What they wanted was protection for their people, room to expand, and lands to increase the value of their financial base.

Just expelled from Nauvoo, Illinois, for practicing polygamy, the Church of Jesus Christ of Latter-day Saints (Mormons), were seeking a new home for their religious base. Brigham Young, president of the Quorum of the Twelve Apostles, had repeatedly asked the US government for assistance and protection, which were never granted.

Faced with war; the protection of a vast, mostly unexplored land; and the need to bind a group of people headed for rebellion, President Polk conceived a plan that would benefit both the United States and the Mormons. Polk did not want the Mormons to join forces with Mexico, and he needed a show of force in the Southwest Territory. Knowing Mexico would attempt to annex California, Polk wanted more troops in that area. The President's goal was to bind the Mormons' loyalty to America and establish the country's claim to the southwest territory. Through negotiations, the two parties reached a compromise.

Polk hoped to achieve his goal of the annexation of southwest lands and California by showing strength. For this tactic he commissioned a Mormon Battalion to march to California. Along their route they were to build a wagon road. This road would eventually become important as routes for the Butterfield Overland Stage trail, the Southern Pacific Railroad, and our modern cross-country highway system.

For Brigham Young the agreement meant an opportunity to show the Mormons' allegiance to the United States, a chance to earn much needed money for their coffers, and an opportunity to explore potentially promising areas for future settlement.

Each Mormon soldier received a uniform allowance of forty-two dollars in advance. Since civilian clothes were allowed, the bulk of these funds went into the general church fund. The church received approximately thirty thousand dollars for the one-year commitment of the Mormon Battalion. Thirty-three women, serving mostly as laundresses, and fifty-one children accompanied the battalion. There were additional funds to pay the laundresses, many of whom were family members.

Polk asked for a battalion of five hundred volunteers to serve in the Mexican War. Since the Mormons refused to kill, Polk promised them they would not have to fire a shot. As it turned out, they did fight in a battle of sorts when a band of raging bulls attacked them in Arizona. The bulls charged the mules and horses and wounded two soldiers. The Mormons shot into the mass of charging animals and managed to kill about a dozen of them, in a skirmish known as "The Battle of the Bulls."

Polk also had another agenda. He wanted a road west, and the Mormons were to create that road for him on their march to California. Albeit, the road was little more than a wagon trail, but this wagon trail was to have great significance on America's development. The trail was the forerunner of our east–west highway and railroad system.

The five hundred–plus members of the Mormon Battalion mustered into service on July 16, 1846. After several weeks of training, they finally started their cross-country march to California. They began their march in Council Bluffs, Iowa. Their circuitous route, led by Lieutenant Colonel Philip St. George Cooke, took them through Missouri, Kansas, New Mexico, and Arizona. Jean Baptiste Charbonneu, the son of Sacagawea, and Pauline Weaver, were their guides.

The battalion arrived in San Diego on January 29, 1847. They performed occupation duties until the end of their commitment, July 14, 1847, when they disbanded. A few reenlisted, some escorted John C. Frémont east to stand court-martial for his mutinous efforts to control California. Some stayed on and found work at Sutter's Mill. Mormon Henry Bigler was actually at the mill on January 24, 1848, the day of the big gold discovery.

The mission of the Mormon Battalion was a success. Polk had the loyalty of the Mormons and he had his wagon road west. The church earned a significant amount of money and demonstrated their allegiance to America. The nineteen-hundred-mile march had introduced the Mormons to the countryside, enabling them to scout out possible settlement sites. Less than ten years later, Brigham Young was calling families to settle on some of this land in what now was the Arizona Territory.

The migrants soon discovered it was an unaccommodating land. The terrain was unforgiving with mountains and canyons making travel difficult. A lot of the agriculture land was rocky and, even when cleared, offered no easy livelihood. The territory offered its own form of torture. Mormon David Kimball and his family, some of the first to settle in this inhospitable land, reported that "water is so scarce one may travel 50 to 60 miles in any direction without finding it."

The Mexican-American War ended in 1847 with America victorious. It gave the United States the right to purchase 26,670 square miles along Mexico's northern border for ten million dollars. The Gadsden Purchase made Polk's dream a reality. It gave America the southern route needed for a transcontinental railroad that would join the United States coast-to-coast.

What the United States had acquired was a land rich in culture, customs, and history. The indigenous people arrived almost a thousand years before, and their decedents were now scattered in wandering tribes and pueblos throughout the land. There were pockets of Mexican villages and large tracts of ranches. The Mexicans' claim to the land came via their forbearers, the Spanish Conquistadors, though by this time they were more Mexican than they were Spanish.

The United States offered the Mexican villagers the option to return to Mexico. Most refused. They preferred to stay, and in doing so became American citizens. This was their home; they were now more Western than Mexican.

Their towns, although small and scattered, contained all the necessities of any rural town . . . stores, doctors, and, of course, saloons. There was even a rough and ready semblance of civilization in the mining towns.

The acquisition of land for a southern railroad route, plus the discovery of gold in California, brought the Southwest to the forefront of the American public's attention. For the business tycoons it meant a railroad west to the gold fields and ports of California. To the average citizen it meant a wild land with Indians and Mexicans, and to the adventuresome, it was an offer, a chance for a different life.

Some say there was no good and bad in the Old West. To them it was all bad, the marauding and massacring Indians, the killer outlaws, and the corrupt politicians; and that didn't include the vicious heat, lack of water, and hazardous terrain. However, these people were wrong. The reality was far more exciting and promising. There was much good in the Old West. There was courage, humor, and a pact with God. The pact was by the lawful and the lawless; it was one of their means of survival.

The remoteness of the land, the rough topography, and the lawlessness made the territory an enticing destination for those who dreamed of a better life and thought they would find an easy life. It wasn't long before the pioneers came.

Some of the prospectors heading out to the California gold fields stopped and stayed, others came back after they found disillusionment in the gold fields of the West Coast. Those looking for land settled and built farms and ranches; entrepreneurs took their business expertise and helped

Pauline Weaver, Arizona pioneer trapper and guide

turn small, sleepy villages into thriving towns and cities. Others, well, they took their advantages either legally or illegally and helped make this new land the Wild West.

THE EARLY ARRIVALS

From 1820 to 1830, the type of men who arrived in the land had different missions and goals than the earlier Conquistadors and European explorers. These were not explorers sent by the government, nor were they soldiers or religious men. They were entrepreneurs—fur trappers. Among them was the father and son team of Sylvester and James Ohio Pattie, Pauline Weaver, Kit Carson, Jedediah Smith, Bill Williams, Michel Robidoux and Antoine Leroux. They trapped around the Gila and San Pedro Rivers for beaver and bear, blazing the trails that future pioneers would follow.

Although the trappers made friends with some of the indigenous Indians, most of the Indians treated them in an unfriendly manner. The bellicose natives stole the trappers hide caches, attacked and killed them, or captured them and tortured them to death. From the very beginning there was no safety zone for the trappers.

They couldn't depend on aid or friendliness from the small Mexican villages. Lawlessness ruled these frontier outposts. The legal law was hundreds of miles away in Mexico City, and except for collecting revenues, had little concern for the actions of the villagers. From the beginning the trappers experienced hostile and life-threatening situations. In one attack, they killed more than two hundred Indians and lost a score of their own party. For four days after that encounter, barefooted, hungry, emaciated, and enduring unbelievable cold, they were on the run. On the fourth day, they managed to kill a raven, and seven men feasted.

The next day they killed a buzzard, and after that an otter supplied their breakfast and supper. Desperate, they finally had to kill one of their dogs for food. Things got better after that. They found a source of water and an area that had abundant wild deer and turkey. Their basic survival needs were not their only worry. They had to be constantly on guard to protect their valuable fur caches.

While James and his father, Sylvester Pattie, were escaping a band of hostile Yuma Indians, Mexican villagers captured and jailed them, holding them for ransom. The conditions were deplor-

Charles D. Poston considered the father of Arizona

able, and Sylvester died of fever. The Mexicans refused to release James, even after he was able to get the town officials and members of his trapper party to locate one of the Pattie fur caches and pay the ransom. What finally earned him his release was an act of nature. A smallpox epidemic broke out in the town. It seems Pattie had in his stash enough vaccine to inoculate the villagers and he did, saving their lives. For that, they let him go.

LIFE ON THE EARLY FRONTIER

Life in the wilderness was not easy for the settlers who followed the trappers west. Living accommodations included dugouts, tents, or poorly constructed cabins. A dugout of a family killed in an Indian raid became the home of Alonzo (Abe) Winsor. It was a simple design about twenty feet long by fifteen feet wide, with a fireplace along the back wall; its only entrance was a doorway in the front wall. The rock walls were about eighteen inches above the ground. A flat roof of juniper poles, loose bark, and dirt kept the dugout waterproof in all but the worse monsoon weather.

As the pioneer men came west to seek their fortunes, the mining towns grew in size, and so did the opportunity for sin. Charleston kept its four saloons going continually. Gambling and "ladies of the night" were busy keeping the prospectors and frontier soldiers happy. As more families migrated, the money from the taxes on bawdy houses and saloons went toward supporting the public school system.

Other than some grocery stores and corrals, most of the businesses in southwestern towns were saloons that were open twenty-four hours a day, seven days a week. Samuel Martin Shook experienced that first-hand when he was six years old and arrived in Prescott with his family on Christmas Eve. His family camped in a wagon yard on the bank of a small creek that ran through the center of town. The main drag was Whiskey Row, and his pa promptly parked himself there and stayed there most of the time they lived in Prescott. The town was wild and wooly, with more than forty saloons and not much else.

A few of the saloons were respectable, but most did business under suspect unethical procedures. Games were as crooked as they could get away with. James Wolf described the dealers as "soft-handed, fishy-eyed, well-dressed, and smooth-spoken." They came from all over the world and were on the run from the law in some country or place. All of the dealers wore .45s, and just in case that didn't work, they had a house gun hidden under the table. Behind them sat a lookout. The lookout was an extra precaution in case of trouble.

Processional gamblers filled the saloons and waited for the cowboys, soldiers, and muleskinners so they could beat them out of their money. One night they invited freighter Abe Winsor into a game. They asked the bartender to give them a deck of cards. The gamblers and the bartender knew what kind of "deck"; they were "strippers." The whole deck was a trifle smaller than the high cards, thus making it easy to pull the high cards out of the pack.

They played with this deck for a while, but they soon discovered that every time it was Abe Winsor's turn to deal, he got the high cards and was getting a little more of the gamblers' money than they were getting of his. One of the gamblers told the bartender to "take this deck of cards away" and to give them another deck. Winsor told them they needn't bother: "I would be ashamed of it if I were you boys, to play with that deck of cards. There isn't a Mormon boy on the Gila River who doesn't know how to play with a deck like that."

The bartender was one of Winsor's friends; he had been with him in many of the mining camps. Joe Winsor, his son, remembers hearing the bartender say to his father, "Abe I wouldn't have handed him that deck of cards but I knew you could play with it as well as they could."

Abe Winsor was quite the gambler. He would stay in town and let his freight teams go on ahead and in a few days overtake them, generally with four or five hundred and sometimes as much as a thousand dollars. The gamblers, cowboys, and freighters were well acquainted with him and had a saying: "Look out for old blind Abe, because he can't see anything except four aces."

Gamblers were a sharp lot in many ways. The second day James Wolf was in Charleston, he entered a saloon for a drink. The faro dealer was having an argument with a customer concerning a bet. The customer left. The faro dealer sat down at the end of the bar and began reading the newspaper. As James finished his drink, he heard someone outside approaching the doorway. The faro dealer tilted back his chair and raised his feet to the bar. Suddenly, though sitting in this awkward position, he reached into his belt with his right hand, pulled out a .45, and dotted the newcomer exactly between the eyes, just as that man arrived in front of the open doorway.

The dead man was the argumentative customer; he had gone to his room for his gun. The dealer didn't move from his chair but went on calmly reading the newspaper, which he held in his left hand, leaving his shooting hand, the right one, free. The gambler's experiences and instinct told him that this man was coming back ready for trouble. It was simply part of his day's work to get in the first shot.

The saloons were small, and if a man passed out during the night, he was usually stuck outside so as not to crowd the remaining customers. Sometimes a man's enemies would discover him and the next day there was a dead man on the street. It was a common sight for early morning workers, to spot one or more bodies lining the road. If a dead man had a gun on him, and the killing shot came from in front of him, no one bothered to look for the killer. They figured it was a fair fight.

Whiskey Row, Prescott, in the 1800s AUTHOR'S COLLECTION

DANGER A DAILY COMPANION

The hostile Indians were a constant danger. It wasn't uncommon for a coworker or friend to say good-bye and head out for another camp, or place, where wages or conditions were better. Usually you never heard from them again. However, too frequently, his outfit showed up in the possession of a captured Apache, or someone found his body on the trail. It was so common that no one got very excited about the news. Sometimes a victim would come barreling into town chased by the Apaches. If he made it into town, he was deemed not seriously hurt, and after a few shots of whiskey, the townsfolk sent him on his way.

Anyone traveling ran the risk of robbery and death at the hands of bandits. Naturally they had to protect themselves. They did it with Colts strapped to their sides. The miners could hold their own in any fisticuffs fight, but with all those guns around, they wouldn't have a chance. Therefore, they too packed firearms. At least that gave them an even chance. Of course, with so many guns, there was bound to be some impulsive behavior. Not all the gunfight winners were the righteous, but they were the fastest.

Although there are accounts of Mexicans, Anglo pioneers, and Native Americans cooperating, for the most part hate ran deep and wide in the Old West. Anglos mistrusted Mexicans, and Mexicans reciprocated the feeling. Both hated the Indians. The Indians viewed the interlopers on their land as enemies who threatened their way of life—and their lives. Racial and ethnic slurs were part of the daily language and did nothing to cool tempers and bring views to a more tolerant level.

There was a deep misunderstanding between the pioneers and the Indians based on suspicion, a suspicion originally founded on a lack of cultural knowledge. In 1874 a posse shot four Navajo braves they *thought* were stealing cattle. Three died, but a fourth made it back to his tribe after a long and painful journey. The Indians swore revenge.

They traveled to the Lee family settlement. The Lees had been fore-warned of the impending attacking by a friendly Navajo. They prepared for the attack by taking in a large supply of wood, digging a well inside the house, and stacking sandbags for the portholes. They cleaned and pre-pared their firearms.

Three days later the Indians arrived and made an offer. They would leave if the settlers gave them three male members of the family. The Indians planned to tie the men to stakes in the front yard of the cabin and burn them. The Lee family refused. The Indians came back with a final offer: They would accept the old invalid miner who was temporarily living with the Lees. Again the family refused.

The Indians surrounded the house and camped out for the night. The Lees realized a siege was about to begin. They decided to send John, their fourteen-year-old son, for help. That night the father slipped out, saddled a horse, and led it to the door. The boy sneaked out of the house, slipped a foot into the stirrup, and was off. Knowing he would be followed, he set up an ambush in a narrow gorge. When the Indians approached, he shot into the faces of the horses, causing them to turn and plunge.

With his own horse wounded, he managed to reach the river at Lee's Ferry. He tried getting the attention of the ferryboat operator but failed. Knowing time was of the essence, he swam the river. On the other side he traveled a mile and a half to his destination, the house of friends. As soon as he arrived, the family immediately sent a message to Utah asking for help.

The next night the boy was ferried across the river. During his ride back home, he came across several hobbled horses. Their Indian owners were sleeping nearby. Cautiously he continued riding through the night, reaching his home at daybreak. The next day the Indians began moving away; they realized the young boy's trip to recruit help was successful and reinforcements would soon arrive.

Not all Indians were hostile to whites. Juan Jose, chief of the Maricopa tribe, rendered invaluable assistance to American immigrants, often supplying them with grain and forage, aiding them in recovering their cattle, and showing in other ways his desire to maintain friendly relations with the Americans. He even went as far as refusing to aid the Mexicans in cutting off General Cooke's command in 1847.

When the Apaches went on the warpath in 1883 and threatened to wipe out Mesa, the Pima and Maricopa Indians formed a line of defense east of the desert and maintained it for days. Fortunately the Apaches never attacked.

Manuel Campas remembers that Geronimo was raiding as late as 1886. He kidnapped a boy from Tanque Verde, north of Tucson, and Mariano Samaniego and several of the local ranchers formed a posse and pursued him. Campas and his father were part of that posse. They rode hard and were able to rescue the boy and recover some of the stolen cattle. Geronimo's attacks ranged all over the territory. On his next raid the Indian chief's band killed a foreman at Morgan's Ranch, near the Empire Ranch, slaughtering the mares and horses.

A PRETTY GIRL CAN CHANGE A MAN

The pioneer men, especially in mining towns, worked at least ten hours a day in backbreaking occupations. They played the same way—hard. They drank, gambled, and danced with the saloon girls. When a new schoolteacher, or a family with daughters, showed up, some of the more romantic and hopeful men would slick their hair down with soap and attend church to get an introduction to the fair lasses. If they got any encouragement at all, even if it was only a smile, the men would invest in an outfit of store clothes, and with every corn aching, dressed in a stiff collar like a government mule, attended the next church bazaar. There they would spend their fortunes on raffle tickets, hoping to win the picnic basket of one of the fair ladies.

MOTHER NATURE CAN BE FEISTY

In case the rough life and the Indians didn't get you, Mother Nature would throw in a kicker, like steaming temperatures or violent monsoon rains. Monsoons were not the only ugly weather pioneers had to face. James G. Wolf knew it was hot, but he got along fine until he saw a thermometer. When he read it was 124 degrees, he realized he was miserable. He "lay off of thermometers" after that. He figured they only made him feel the heat more.

In 1887 it was more than a kicker Mother Nature threw in, it was an earthquake. James Wolf was there to experience it all.

I was over in the Huachuca Mountains on May 2, when suddenly all the ground around me commenced to ripple and wave. It rose in billows to a height of two or three feet and would then drop in the same place, but leaving pronounced cracks. The rocky ledges along the sides of the Huachuca's rose up and fell outward, breaking into all sizes of boulders that rolled down the mountainsides, snapping off trees and brush that were in their path. The friction of the rocks set fire to the grass and pretty soon, not only the Huachuca's, but also the Dragoon and San Jose mountains burst into flames.

I could see deer, coyotes, and rabbits running from the hills. The wild cattle along the San Pedro, who had never known what fear was before, just stuck their tails straight into the air, and with eyes popping out, beat it for elsewhere, no two of them in the same direction. The ground was heaving all around and there was nothing to indicate where a really safe refuge was to be found, but you could see their main idea was to be somewhere else immediately. I felt exactly the same way. I suddenly remembered there was some business I had forgotten to attend to. Besides, I was all out of rattlesnake cure. I felt the need of some right then.

They told me the quake was about twenty minutes in duration, but you could not prove it by me. I was well on my way long before that. There was no telling how many poisonous reptiles might be forced out of their holes by this eruption, so I hurried to get to town before the medicine was all gone.

On my way to Charleston from the Huachuca's, I saw sheets of water spurting into the air at many places as I neared the river. Later I learned from others this had occurred in hundreds of places on both sides of the river, and for its entire length. The quake shattered rock strata and the underground water escaped through the fissures. Some of these new springs flowed only a short time. A few flowed for about a month, and a very few even longer than that. However, there were so many of them they eventually drained all the upper country of its reservoirs of stored water.

Every day, and at the same hour, for about a month, the earth's trembling recurred, but with gradually lessened force, and for a shorter duration each time, until finally they faded away to nothing. Mules, cows, and horses would stop and brace their legs. Their eyes would become round and glassy in appearance. A gentle hush would come over them. Then, the trembler would come.

Water is a precious commodity in Arizona, especially in the southwest. Untold numbers of pioneers died from lack of it. It was not unusual for springs to dry up and popular water holes to disappear. You never knew when a previously reliable water hole might go dry. Travelers and freighting outfits would arrive at a supposedly good watering place at nightfall to find not a drop of water.

Everybody carried a canteen, and the wagons always had a keg or two of water. If the travelers came to a dry water hole, the keg water was sparingly doled out, and the outfit would push on the next day to the next water, which they might find also dry. If so, their only choice was to continue on, still uncertain if they would find precious water ahead. Occasionally an entire outfit perished from thirst.

EVEN WATER CAN PROVIDE A LAUGH

The abundance of negative factors working against the pioneer men produced some unique character traits, among them an outrageous sense of humor, ingenuity, and courage. The men also had a laissez-faire attitude about life, doing what they could and accepting what they couldn't control. The men could find humor even when it came to precious water. The earthquake produced such a situation.

In the beginning of the Tombstone camp, drinking water was brought up from the San Pedro River. Then a small supply of water was found outside town, and the spot was named Watervale. The Watervale Water Company was formed, and through reservoirs, tanks, boilers, and a supply pipeline, it delivered water to town. Soon the Watervale's water supply proved to be inadequate for the needs of the pioneers.

Two men, Dick Gird and his partner M. M. O'Gorman, formed the Huachuca Water Company. They built dams in the Huachuca Mountains and piped good water to Tombstone, a distance of over twenty-five miles.

The Watervale Water Company continued to exist and seemed to strike new and better strata of water, frequently increasing their quantity. There were two sets of water pipes in every street, one for each company. The competition was fierce and annoying.

When the earthquake ripped through Tombstone, it damaged the underground water pipes. The Huachuca Company set about repairing their pipes, which were under terrific pressure, as their source was high up in the distant mountains. During the repair work, the Huachuca Water Company discovered a secret connection from their supply line to the pipes of the Watervale Water Company's system. All this time the Huachuca Water Company had been supplying water to the Watervale Water Company's pipe system, filling up all their tanks and reservoirs.

The Huachuca Water Company sued, claiming all the money the Watervale Water Company had received over the years from their sales. The Watervale Water Company denied all knowledge of the existence of the unauthorized pipe connects and was appropriately shocked. In the style of the Old West, no one bothered to think of the ethics or lack of them in stealing water. In typical frontier humor, they all had a good laugh when they thought about the Huachuca Water Company furnishing water to its rival . . . free of charge.

CHAPTER 1

Outlaws and Lawmen

Two Six Shooters Beat Four Aces

—John Ringo

It was the "law of the gun" in the West, and the man who was handy with firearms, in 1880, could use his skill to earn money. Most did, even if it meant jumping over the fine line of the law. The law had no problem hiring a gunman who was an outlaw to help apprehend another outlaw. The premise being, "It takes a thief to catch a thief."

So many men went armed in the frontier's golden days that the only way you could tell who was the outlaw was to see who was pointing the gun at the bank teller. That day, he was an outlaw. The next day, however, the gunman could be wearing a badge and bringing in the rustlers. This added not only to the difficulty in enforcing the law, but many times pitted friend against friend.

The Laws of the West were rather simple:

1. A lawman today might be an outlaw tomorrow.
2. Never trust a stranger.
3. Shootouts and killings are a part of life.
4. Frontier justice is quick, decisive, and not always fair.

LAWMAN TODAY, OUTLAW TOMORROW

One of the strangest friendships lawman Ignacio Calvillo had was with Bert Alvord. Alvord had served as a deputy sheriff under John Slaughter and that is when Calvillo and Alvord became friends. Later on Alvord ranched around Wilcox and lived the life of a respectable citizen. Then again, a man never could tell about a fellow by his face and circumstances.

Calvillo saw nothing strange about Bert Alvord stopping by his ranch to buy horses. Calvillo was more than willing to make a sale; unfortunately, he didn't have any horses for sale. Since Alvord was willing to pay seventy-four dollars for each horse, and he was a friend, Calvillo told him he would check around with the other ranchers.

It turned out that old man Marsh Driscoll, another cattleman, had some stock for sale, and he and Alford struck a bargain. Driscoll agreed to deliver the horses to Benson.

Two days later Alvord, Billy Stiles, and Three-Finger Jack held up a train at Fairbanks. Jeff Milton, the Wells Fargo agent, was shot in the holdup. Sheriff Scott White and his deputies mounted a posse and went after the train robbers, but Alvord and his partners got away on their newly purchased horses.

Alvord disappeared for a while, and no one heard anything about him until Calvillo went to Old Mexico on a visit. There in Cananea he saw a man named Tomas Gonzales sitting in the back corner of a store. The man's complexion was weather beaten and his body wrapped in a serape, with his sombrero pulled down low; he was almost impossible to recognize.

Frank Stevens, the store's owner, came into the store, followed by some lawmen. They explained that they had heard Bert Alvord had taken refuge across the border and they wanted to know if Stevens had seen him. Now Stevens was not a lawyer, just a man of the Old West. The man in the corner said he was Tomas Gonzales, and that was good enough for Stevens. He told the officers he had not seen Alvord. When the lawmen left, Stevens, Calvillo, and Alvord (Gonzales) had a good laugh. Calvillo may have served as a law officer at times, but in Mexico, he was just another visitor.

The lawmen, however, were not ready to give up and came up with a plan to trap Alvord. One day a Mexican outlaw met with Alvord and proposed they rob a certain ranch on the US side of the border. Alvord went along with the plan even though he didn't quite trust the Mexican.

When they arrived at the ranch that night, they found it deserted. The Mexican insisted the money was inside the ranch house and told Alvord exactly where he could find it. The Mexican said he would remain outside on guard. However, Alvord was not about to enter the house, and with a steely glint in his eye, he ordered the Mexican to go get the money; after all he was the one who knew exactly where it was. Not given any other choice, the Mexican entered the ranch house and met with a volley of shots. Alvord figured right and in grim satisfaction rode away in the night.

Billy Stiles, a partner of Bert Alvord, was also a deputy sheriff at one time. His deputy's duties didn't stop him from joining Alvord and organizing a gang of train robbers, horse thieves, murderers, and cattle rustlers around Pearce and Wilcox.

Bert Alvord served as deputy sheriff and outlaw, sometimes at the same time.
COURTESY LEGENDS OF AMERICA

Being part lawman and part outlaw had its advantages. In 1903 Alvord and Stiles were in the Tombstone jail for holding up a Southern Pacific train near Cochise and robbing the Wells Fargo Express Company. They worked as jailors there on and off for years, and they knew every brick in the building. They began removing the mortar from between the bricks in their cell and secretly mixed it with the floor dirt in the jail, or threw it outside through the barred windows. Finally the night came when they had enough bricks loosened to let a man crawl through the opening.

Knowing how deputies and jailers operated, they realized what a fine easy mark they would make when halfway out of the opening. The two argued: Stiles wanted Alvord out first, Alvord thought Stiles should go first. Stiles finally solved the difficulty by grabbing a Mexican who was a material witness in another case and shoving him through the gap. They heard no shots or shouts, so they squeezed through the hole to freedom. They told the Mexican to get out of there.

The Mexican left on a run, but it was a cold morning, and he missed the warm jail. Then he remembered the free meals and the many days of witness fees owed him by the county at $3.50 per day. The first the sheriff's office knew they were shy two very important prisoners was when the Mexican appeared at the front door demanding to be readmitted.

NEVER TRUST A STRANGER

Because the law of the land was determined by who was the fastest, most accurate shot, and you never knew what would trigger a reaction, men learned early not to trust strangers.

Charles Poston and Raphael Pumpelly were trying to reach California. They left Arivaca, Arizona, loaded with silver from the mine they had recently closed down. They headed for Mexico to catch a ship to California. In Caborca, Mexico they found out their ship had been delayed. Their only choice was to push on to Fort Yuma, two hundred miles northeast.

It was a dangerous journey through a wildness known for robber and Indian attacks, so they were more than glad when Jack Williams, a man they had just met, agreed to travel with them to strengthen their party.

They heard rumors that Fort Yuma had closed down, but decided to continue their journey. It was with great relief they found the fort still functioning. They rested at the fort, preparing for their continuing journey west. While there, One-Eyed Jack arrived, and he immediately joined up with Jack Williams. You couldn't miss One-eyed. He was a notorious cutthroat who wore trousers with one white leg and one black leg. It was evident from the way Williams greeted One-Eyed that they had a long-term acquaintance.

On the day of departure from the fort, Poston, Pumpelly, and Williams left the ferry and traveled a mile or so along the Colorado River. When Williams, who the other two hardly knew, disappeared, they became suspicious. They undertook a stealthy search and discovered Williams in some willows holding a conference with One-Eyed Jack. Obviously an ambush was planned.

Poston and Pumpelly altered their plans and headed for a nearby immigrant camp to spend the night. In the morning, as they were about to leave, Williams rode up. Immediately he sensed the distrust and began to mutter threats. Poston was the first to draw, saying, "Williams, the last man you killed has not been dead long enough. We don't wish to shoot you, for we haven't time for buying your kind. Keep the horse and outfit we gave you, but go back and join One-eyed Jack down by the river. You and he cannot kill us for our silver."

Williams's demeanor changed as he dissolved into hearty laughter. He shook hands with the men declaring, "Give us your hand, you're damn sharp." Off he rode, waving his hat and shouting, "Good-bye, Pals, bully for you. You'll do for the border."

VIOLENCE, A PART OF EVERYDAY LIFE

It was a respectable town, a good place for families; however, these attractions did not protect children from witnessing the violence of the frontier. The town of Snowflake had broad streets, thriving businesses, and prosperous agricultural fields. Sheriff William J. Flake was a prominent businessman, a Mormon bishop, and the postmaster. When this responsible man received a telegraph wire from Holbrook and Fort Apache, he immediately set about to do his duty.

It was 1893 and a stranger had recently arrived in Snowflake, taking lodging with a widow lady. Strangers were always suspect, and this one did little to change that. He was never without his guns, and he always kept his horse saddled, even in the barn. He was also mysterious in his movements. He never stood near a door or window. He hung around the barroom of the local saloon and the pool hall, making money by betting on his marksmanship. He could hit a dollar tossed into the air with his six shooter.

When the telegraph arrived describing the stranger, Sheriff W. J. Flake brought his brother, armed with a Winchester, along with him to arrest the man. They went to the boarding house and called out for the man. When the outlaw came to the door, the sheriff and his deputy announced they were there to arrest him. He broke between them and made a run for the barn and his saddled horse.

The two officers grabbed the outlaw and seized his right arm, but the gunman was clever with both hands. He drew another six-gun with his left hand, swung his arm across his body, pointed the gun over his right shoulder, and pulled the trigger. The bullet cut the jugular vein of Sheriff Flake, striking him down.

The gunman broke away from the deputy and ran like hell for the barn. As he ran, he fired again, and a bullet just nicked the ear of Deputy Flake as he raised his 30-30. The deputy took a bead on the running man and fired just once. The bullet entered the exact center of the outlaw's head and emerged from the front, killing him instantly. Someone put a hat over the outlaw's shattered face as the body lay on the ground.

School had just let out, and around the corner trooped a group of schoolboys. Boys being boys, they had to lift the hat and peek at the outlaw's shattered head. Mothers and fathers began shooing the children away from the killings.

Snowflake went into mourning for their sheriff and the outlaw. The women of the town said the outlaw was some mother's son and maybe she loved him. The outlaw and the sheriff got the same eulogy and an equal send-off to heaven, or wherever their destination.

Perhaps John Hunt formed an attitude about outlaws when, as a boy, he witnessed the hanging of Jim Stott, Jimmie Scott, and Jeff Wilson for stealing horses. It was not a pleasant experience for a boy, especially since Scott's friends insisted the law had hung an innocent man.

Hunt's first experience with Jim Stott came when his father had sent him to the Stott ranch to look for some missing horses. He went to the ranch hoping to get information about the horses—and an invitation to spend the night, as he had ridden all day and was tired. Arriving just before sundown, he found the ranch deserted. He waited a few minutes, but then decided to ride on.

Hunt had gone only a few miles when he came to a small opening in the timbers. Through it he saw a large open space surrounded by tall pines and thick underbrush. There he spotted Jim Stott and his partner, Red Holcomb. They had staked out two old mares with heavy irons so that they couldn't run. With the mares were about fifteen colts.

Hunt had heard rumors about the number of horses increasing fast on the Stott at ranch. Realizing the danger he was in if he were caught, he rode away as quietly as he could.

Afterward Hunt found out Stott and Holcomb would gather up a bunch of colts and keep them in this enclosure with the two old mares until weaned. Then they would brand them and turn them loose on the range, claiming them as part of their stock. After a time the rustlers were not content to get just the colts. They actually came and stole fine work teams right out of the stables, taking them to the Salt River and selling them.

Even family gatherings were not immune to the violence that permeated the West. In 1902 Joe Winsor, his wife, and their two children headed for a dance in town. Families from all over the area came to share in the fun. At the dance parents deposited their babies in a room that had several beds. The floor manager disarmed the guests as they came into the dance and stacked the weapons in the room with the babies. The pile of guns was so high, a grown man couldn't jump over it.

The dance was open to everyone, and that included Bronco Bill and his gang. The floor manager tried to take Bronco Bill's guns, and he did hand over one of them. The floor manager called him out, "You've got another one there, Bill, give it to me." The outlaw replied, "No, that's one I never give to nobody."

Desiring to avoid trouble, the floor manager let it go, and everyone entered and started dancing. About midnight Bronco Bill asked a Mexican girl to dance with him. She told him she had promised that dance to someone else, to which Bronco Bill shouted, "When the Mexican women won't dance with me I'll be damned if anybody else will dance."

He jerked out his six shooter and shot at the lights. One wise constable got out of that room and broke for home. By the time Bronco Bill had finished shooting, the dance had broken up and nobody was in sight. Parents found their own, or somebody else's, kids and started for home.

Lawmen at Fort Thomas went hunting for Bronco Bill and his gang of outlaws. The morning after the dance, Bronco Bill and his gang headed for the White Mountains. Leaving Fort Thomas, Sheriff Stillman and his deputies followed the gang. They caught up with them at Black River, and the shootout that followed killed several deputies and wounded Bronco Bill. When they brought the outlaw into the hospital, they found him shot all to pieces. However, he was a tough hombre and survived only to be convicted of his crimes.

Steal It, Rob It, or Shoot It

Western outlaws operated under a simple principle: If it moved, you robbed it. If you couldn't rob it, you stole it, and if you couldn't steal it, well, you would just have to shoot it. That seems to sum up all their depredations.

The most popular crime in Arizona in the 1800s was rustling livestock. The claiming of cattle off the range had an innocent enough start. Wild beeves and horses freely roamed the grassy plains. They were the decedents of the abandoned cattle brought over by Father Kino and the Spanish in the 1500s.

Even though wild cattle were scrawny and difficult to handle, with them independent cowboys saw an opportunity to enhance, or start, their own herds by rounding up calves without brands and setting their own brand on the hides. Impatient rustlers, who didn't want to wait for the livestock to grow up, used a running iron to alter the brands cattle already bore and claiming the cattle as their own.

Of course market-ready cattle produced a quicker income, and soon there was a trade in stealing from ranches in the north and selling them in the south, then reversing the process. They would steal horses and cattle from the Mormons, sell them in southern Arizona, then steal southern cattle, and sell them to the Mormons in the north.

The rustlers were indiscriminate and ruthless. Legitimate ranchers did not appreciate this get-rich-quick initiative at their expense, so they and the law went after the rustlers. This action resulted in shoot-outs, hangings, prison time, and death on both sides of the law.

Joe Winsor and his father, Abe, got a chance to witness this lucrative business firsthand when they were hauling lumber from the Chihuahua Mountains into Tombstone. Eight miles out of Tombstone, the Clanton Brothers stole all the Winsors' horses and left them afoot. George Adair and Abe Winsor went into Tombstone to get help from Sheriff Wayne Earp. However, Earp refused to aid the men. Convinced that Earp was afraid of the Clantons, both Winsor and Adair decided to go after the rustlers. Winsor bought a buckskin mule and a bay horse, and they set out after the Clantons.

Following the trail, they came upon the rustler's still-warm fire and knew they were close to them. Winsor spotted a pipe lying near the fire, and picking it up he announced, "Well, I'll take that son of a bitch's pipe to him anyhow."

Early the next day Adair was riding in the lead. "Abe," he called, "there are a couple of fellows there under a tree. What shall we do?"

A determined and pragmatic Winsor replied, "We will ride straight to them, but don't pull your gun."

They rode up to the men who were asleep under a cedar tree. They called out to the sleepers and woke them up. The outlaws jumped up with their Winchesters in their hands. Winsor told the outlaws they were hunting bulls. Since the freighters used many bull teams, this explanation was readily accepted. The rustlers told the two men to head out for their camp and told them how to get there.

On their way Winsor and Adair ran into two more men. "Abe, there come two fellows riding up through the sand wash, and they have got their guns on us, what shall we do?" Winsor replied, "We will ride right up to them, but don't pull your gun."

When they got closer to the men, the outlaws took their guns down. They talked for a while, and eventually the outlaws invited Winsor and Adair over to their camp and told them they could stay all night.

Sitting around the campfire during supper, one of the outlaws remarked, "I wish my pal would come in. I haven't had a smoke since I lost my pipe."

Winsor reached into his pocket and pulled out his own pipe and the one he found. "I have two pipes. I'll give you one. Take your choice." The outlaw picked his own pipe declaring, "I lost that and didn't know just where I lost it yesterday." Winsor and Adair decided to make an exit as soon as possible, before the outlaw figured out how Abe got his pipe.

At one point, the Clanton members were brought into court and they recognized George Adair, who had been summoned as a witness against them. That's when Winsor and Adair decided to leave town. They had learned a long time ago that it was useless to try to get any assistance from the law in bringing rustlers to justice.

In the late 1800s Ignacio Calvillo served as a ranger when Arizona was struggling as a territory and hoping for statehood. Rustling was on the rise, and lawmen were losing the battle. Cattle thieves were bold and innovative. Some of the cow thieves killed the beeves and brought them into Ray, selling them to the butchers.

One day, out on the range, Calvillo found a calf tied up and decided to watch it to see if anything happened. Soon Lee Cutworth and three other cow thieves rode up. They killed the calf and brought it into the butcher shop in Ray. Calvillo decided to let it go this time. When he found one of his cattle missing, and discovered the beef hid in an old tunnel and the hide dumped in an old well, he changed his mind and was now ready to do something about these thieves.

Sheriff Henry Hall told Calvillo that there were some cattle up in the slaughter pen and it wouldn't be a bad idea for him to see what was in there. He rode up to the pen and found a bunch of steers that the Campbell boys had brought in from Florence.

There were two big cows and a two-year-old heifer that Calvillo knew had not been sold. He knew because they belonged to the Gibson boys, who ran their stock with his cattle. They wore the F brand. He stayed and watched until the last one in the pen was killed, then he arrested Lee Cutworth, Frank Campbell, and his brother Johnny, who were running a butcher shop in Sonora.

He took the boys down to the butcher shop and asked them to show him the bill of sale that Lee Cutworth had given the Campbell boys for the cattle. Sure enough, the bill of sale did not show the F Gibson brand. Calvillo found that the butcher shops of Sonora and Ray stood in with the rustlers. He arrested them all and hauled them off to Florence, where they were sentenced to two to five years.

The only one that ever served a term was Lee Cutworth. He put in two years, and as soon as he got out, he began selling horses, more horses, and more horses until he went back into the penitentiary. Every time he got out, he would do some more devilment. He spent the biggest part of twenty years in the pen.

When Calvillo next rode through Ray, some of the citizens told him his cow thieves, who were now prisoners, had just ridden though town on their way to work on the road that the state was building. Governor George W. P. Hunt was putting this little road through the Pinal Mountains. They were building it with state prisoners.

During this time, the rangers captured a lot of bad men and convicted them. However, they never did serve their terms. Governor Hunt would let them out. Finally, disgusted with this process, a group of rangers and deputies got together and decided to shoot, and then holler, "Halt." They didn't bring in many outlaws from then on.

While livestock rustling was the most prolific of crimes, it was not the only one perpetrated in the Old West. Pedro Perez remembers Jack Suelar as one of the most active robbers between 1865 and 1900. Suelar and his partner, Jose Duran, lived in El Salado, now called Phoenix. They were the Robin Hoods of their time, robbing stages and express shipments, and generously sharing their loot with the poor. Because of their generosity, no one in town would confront them. They continued their criminal ways until they realized that things were changing, and maybe it was time for them to retire. Congress was in the process of passing laws that eliminated the "law of the gun," which prevailed in the West.

Suelar retired to his ranch in Agua Fria, and even though he became a law-abiding citizen, he found he was not exonerated from past deeds. Years later, arrested for past murders and robberies, and convicted of his crimes, he died an old man in Yuma Prison. Jose Duran turned out to be the smarter of the two. He retired in Old Mexico, taking his ill-gotten loot with him.

Nothing was more tempting to a potential robber than a mine. Watching the ore brought out of the tunnels was enough to get the blood of every get-rich-easy bandit pumping. While some mines looked like easy pickings, few robberies were successful. In 1887 two men robbed the Vulture gold mine shipment. The Mexican bandits killed Captain Gribble and his four bodyguards while they were on their way to Phoenix with the gold. Gribble, recalled Ignacio Calvillo, was the mine superintendent. They got away with thirty-eight thousand dollars in gold, and a posse went after the bandits.

Clever in the robbery, they showed less sense in their getaway. Weary and sleepy, they stopped at the junction of the Hassayampa and Gila Rivers to sleep. They used the bags of stolen gold for pillows. They never awoke, and the posse recovered the loot.

Charleston, a rich mining town, was the ideal place for a holdup. For miles to the west and north, it was an Apache infested area. To the south lay Old Mexico, where a few petty larceny officials would protect American bandits—for a consideration. Flowing alongside Charleston was the San Pedro River.

Immediately after a holdup, the bandits could head for the river, where the stream removed all traces of their tracks. Alternatively, they could get a good start by following the river up or down and then leave it at some rocky ledge where the horses' hoofs left no prints. The numerous creeks and washes that emptied into the San Pedro had banks sufficiently high to hide a man on horseback until he was a long ways away.

Mines and banks were prime targets for bandits. Wherever there was money, it served as a magnet for the unlawful. Shortly after James Wolf arrived in Charleston in 1883, the furious tooting of the mill's steam whistle woke him. The whistle blew only for fires and bandits, and since he could see no smoke, he knew it wasn't a fire. He carefully and calmly approached the mill, although he had a great yearning to stay in his room, as it was one of the best and stoutest buildings in Charleston. Then he pictured the bandits seizing the building, using it as a fort if they were hard-pressed.

Wolf joined the crowd running toward the mill. Some men in the crowd carried .45s, others rifles and shotguns, and the rest had picked up anything they could find that might be useful in a free-for-all. As the crowd neared the office, they could see the bandits running for their horses. Although the miners emptied their guns at the bandits, the culprits made it to the river and escaped.

The outlaws had entered the office on some potential business and ordered the bookkeeper to open the safe. Knowing the safe contained little if any real value, he probably thought to detain the bandits and aid in their capture by slow compliance. He was too slow, and the bandits killed him. It was that shot that aroused the mill men, and they tooted the warning whistle.

The bandits got nothing. Blood found near the river meant the mob's bullets found one or more of them, even at that long range, but the bandits were never captured.

Many men, such as Jack Swilling, served two masters. Swilling was a public benefactor to some, a public enemy to others. Old Arizonians, who often accepted his hospitality, refused to believe his accusers. Others, remembering the bloodshed he caused when intoxicated, withheld their sympathies. His contradictory behaviors lead to these conflicting opinions. He cowhided a man for slandering a lady in his presence, but in the end he paid for his outlaw ways. Accused of stage robbery, the law incarcerated him in the Yuma County Jail, where he died on August 12, 1878.

Swilling was not a stranger to jails. He was one of the first prisoners in the mud jail in Tucson. However, this time when arrested, he was in poor health, suffering from fifteen years of exposure and hardship and habitual use of opiates. Because of his weakened condition, the doctor decided to keep him on opiates until he was stronger. The day before his death, he was taking opium in its solid form. After three o'clock in the morning, he fell into a sleep from which he never recovered.

Swilling and Andrew Kirby stood accused of robbing the mail near Wickenburg. However, there were no witnesses. The only evidence against them was the fact that they were in Wickenburg the day the mail left. The citizens of Wickenburg were not friends of Swilling and were willing to believe the worst of him. They still remembered the day he shot up the town.

"The Texan" was another outlaw who took to robbing stages. His actions made him a legend. At one time he worked as a ranch hand for Bob Leatherwood. Leatherwood was later sheriff of Pima County, from 1895 to 1898. As a sideline, The Texan robbed stages as they went around the mountains west of Tucson. The authorities suspected The Texan of the robberies, and Sheriff Charles Shibell went hunting for him.

The outlaw had a hideout on Cat Mountain (Sierrita de Gato), the peak by the Tucson Ajo Road. He hired a man by the name of Davis, who had a ranch in the area, to buy groceries for him and take them to the tunnel where he was hiding.

Davis was a big man with a large moustache to match. His movements were under suspicion, and some fellows figured if they could get him to talk, he might know a lot about stage robberies. Therefore, they got him drunk. When Davis was drunk, a circus barker couldn't outtalk him.

He was offered a ten-thousand-dollar reward if he would take the officers to The Texan's hideout. His eyes glittered with greed. He considered right then and there that he was a law-abiding citizen first and a robber's friend afterward.

He took Sheriff Shibell and deputies, which included James Lee and Charlie Brown. Lee and Brown took positions behind the rocks and bushes at the entrance of the tunnel. Davies and The Texan had arranged a signal of communication. One shot meant that it was safe for The Texan to come out, more than one meant danger. On the day Davies sold out The Texan, he fired one shot. The Texan came out in the open and met a volley from the many muzzles aimed at him; his body dropped, riddled with holes. There were many searches made in an effort to discover where The Texan had hid his loot. Now and then one would hear that two or three different fellows found a cached bag or box of treasure buried in different places.

One of the most lucrative targets was the army payroll. That is if you were willing to try your luck against the soldiers. Apparently, eight men including Old Man Webb, W. T. Webb, Lyon Folette, Ed Folette, Wal Folette, Dave Rodgers, and a man by the name of Cunningham were willing to try their luck.

In 1889 Joe Winsor and eight men were on a cattle drive that took the route from Cottonwood to Bear Springs, then onto the stage road from Fort Grant to Fort Thomas. The next day they learned that the paymaster, J. W. Wham of the US Army was robbed. The eight-thousand-dollar payroll was for the soldiers at Fort Grant, Fort Carlos, and Fort Apache.

Eleven soldiers, including a sergeant leader, escorted the paymaster. The gunmen succeeded in wounding five soldiers and killing the lead mule. The place of the robbery was the old stage road to Cottonwood Springs in the southern part of Graham County. The spot is known as Wham Hill.

The outlaws built a lot of dummies to make it appear that there was a large group of robbers. Some of the soldiers were so badly frightened that they quit their horses and ran all the way to Fort Thomas, thirty miles away. When they finally apprehended the robbers, their trial lasted for a year. Nearly every family in the Gila Valley reported to Tucson as witnesses before the trial was over.

The train first arrived in Arizona in 1877, when the line from California extended across the Colorado River to Yuma. In 1880 the train arrived in Tucson, and shortly after that, completed rails connected the country from coast to coast. The train brought more than passengers to Arizona; it brought freight, and another way to make easy money—train robberies.

Living in Duncan during the late 1890s was a well-known outlaw by the name of Lee Stein. He was with King Hunt and Billy Grounds when the gang murdered seventeen Mexicans and robbed them of their gold bullion in the Skeleton Canyon massacre.

Stein operated alone after coming to Duncan Valley. A gambler, rustler, and killer, he had friends in Duncan, or at least those who knew him well enough to keep "still" about his past. He was a man who took advantage of every opportunity.

In 1904 he held up the mail train at Stein's Pass. Snatching the mail sacks, he tossed them into the top of a tall cactus. He held the train crews at bay by making them think he had an army with him by firing his two Colts so fast from point to point. As soon as the train crew thought the "gang of bandits," was gone, the crew fled. They reported the incident at Bowie, and a posse was immediately formed and on the trail of the bandit.

They found Stein wounded and out of ammunition, but they saw no evidence of the mail sacks. Stein said they would find the sacks where he had tossed them, that he hadn't been able to get back to them.

They arrested Stein, tied his hands behind him, and set him on his own horse. When they came to a narrow rock-walled canyon, Stein's horse bolted and headed up the crooked canyon. The posse started firing, but Stein's zigzag path made it difficult to hit him. He disappeared in the rocky canyon and has never been seen or heard from since. The posse found the mail sacks right where Stein said they would be, in a tall cactus. They were empty.

Individuals were always fair game to robbers, especially if there was evidence they had some money. If you were smart, you took unusual precautions to outwit the robbers, just in case one or more had you marked for a holdup.

James Wolf was not going to let anyone sneak up on him at night. The site of his ranch on the San Pedro, between Lewis Springs and Charleston, made a perfect hideout and a supply point for gang operations along the border. You approached it from up or down the river, and the water left no trail. The high banks of the river, and the washes that drained into it, nicely hid any riders.

Wolf's pasture surrounding the house and the barn was fenced in. The only gate to it was close to the house, yet far enough away to keep some people at a desirable distance. Every night Wolf secretly fastened a piece of twine to the gate and threaded it through a window to his bed, where he would fasten it to his wrist before he went to sleep. If the gate was opened, the twine tugged on Wolf's wrist, waking him up.

Abe Winsor was also wise to the ways of bandits. He, John Kenney, and Ted Adams were hauling supplies around Flagstaff for the railroad. The freighters had trouble getting their pay, and Winsor refused to unload until he got his money. After being paid, they started back home, when suddenly Winsor said, "We better put this money in one of these water barrels, the rustlers are pretty bad and there are hold-ups along here every day."

Sure enough, they hadn't gone far when some men walked out of the pine trees and held them up. They searched Winsor first and took five or ten dollars from him. Then they took away Ted Adams's money, which amounted to about ten dollars. Next they robbed John Kenney, who had a harelip. They gave him the boot and gave him his money back, figuring he had enough trouble. After the bandits left, the freighters moved on. Making camp that night, they decided they had better check the money in their water barrel.

They took the water barrel down but didn't hear any money rattling. They shook it and listened, nothing. Winsor's first thought was that the bandits had seen them putting the money in the barrel and had robbed it the night before. They got out the ax and busted open the barrel. When the barrel split there were their silver coins embedded in about a foot of mud.

Charles Gordes lived at a time when a lot of men wore the label "outlaw." Most of the ones he knew were bad only when under the influence of liquor. There was nothing romantic about them, most of their so-called bravery and thrilling deeds were accidental rather than intentional. However, there were a few men such as John Slaughter and the Earps who earned the respect of the frontier men.

Gordes was in Bisbee with a roll of several hundred dollars to pay off a debt. At the local saloon he asked where he could find his man. While at the saloon, he made a small purchase and foolishly took out his roll to pay.

While getting directions, he noticed a tough-looking face peering in the doorway. To be safe he stuck the money roll up his sleeve, just under the cuff. That day he had purchased a pair of soft baby shoes for a friend's baby. He stuck the shoes, wrapped in a piece of tissue paper, in his pocket.

It was a black night and he could see nothing beyond a foot ahead. Suddenly he felt something hard thrust in his ribs, and a harsh voice said, "Hands up." He raised his hands and felt someone go through his pockets. He thought there were three of them, but the only clue he had was that one smelled strongly of iodine.

Gordes had thirty-five cents, which they soon found. Feeling in Gordes's pocket, one of the bandits said, "Here it is boys." He had found the baby shoes. Grabbing the package, the bandits let Gordes go. He didn't know if they used a gun or a stick in his ribs.

The next night Gordes was at a saloon in Bisbee. Three men walked up to the bar and laid down thirty-five cents for drinks. Seeing the money, and smelling the strong odor of iodine, he asked them if that was his thirty-five cents. Their faces got a funny look; they turned on their heels and walked out. He never had a chance to ask them about the baby shoes.

FRONTIER JUSTICE

When Jim Burnett was the justice of the peace in Charleston, justice on the frontier was quick, decisive, and not always fair. Burnett had no time for frivolous action. He dispensed Justice on the dot. He was prompt and decisive. He could and did hold court anywhere without the aid of a clerk, courtroom, law books, or sissy records. Judge Burnett carried, and could use, a .45 with speed and precision, hence there was a vast amount of law, and some semblance of order, in his vicinity at all times.

James Wolf had a chance to see Judge Burnett in action. A Mexican stole a horse from Mr. Curry. Some days later the Mexican man came into town with a train of wagons loaded with firewood, drawn by a long team of horses. Mr. Curry immediately recognized his horse and proceeded to claim him. As the two men were arguing, Judge Burnett came along. "Is this your horse? Here take him." The judge turned to the thief, "I fine you nine cords of wood to be delivered to the Gird mill." Court had convened and adjourned all in one breath. The Mexican could not argue. His wagons held nine cords of wood, as the judge's trained eyes well knew. The mill got the wood and paid Judge Burnett for the load.

Constable Sam Starr teamed up with Judge Burnett, and they dispensed justice for a good many years around the Charleston area. When a ruckus occurred, the two would go together to the scene. Starr would slip around and get the offenders covered with a shotgun or pistol. Judge Burnett would step forward, open court, and fine the culprits. The court cost would always be as much as if the culprit had been in custody for a month and the court had been in session for that whole time. If rioters prepared for the coming of Starr and Burnett, these two officials turned around and left that infraction of the law for the local deputy sheriff to sort out.

The constable and the judge answered a call to take care of a saloon proprietor who was drunk and loudmouthed. The judge proclaimed, "The fine will be fifty dollars." When the fine was paid, the judge joined the poker game and promptly lost the fifty dollars. The constable knew what he had to do. He started a new argument with the proprietor, who was fined a second time. The second fifty dollars went the way of the first. This time when the constable approached the proprietor, the man started blowing out the lights and then announced the saloon was closing. He was careful to keep his mouth clamped shut near the constable.

The county officials decided to audit Judge Burnett's books. When told of their purpose, Burnett's reply was comprehensive and complete: "Gentlemen, this is a self sustaining office. I never ask anything from the County, and I never give the County anything." Burnett kept no records nor locked up any crooks; the officials went home empty-handed.

A sad state of affairs existed in Cochise County. The jail was full of offenders, and the first laws of the land were full of loopholes. Spellbinding orators like Mark Smith and Al English easily swayed juries, and there were very few convictions secured. Things got so bad the business community decided to take things into its own hands; they convinced John Slaughter to run for sheriff.

Slaughter lived at the extreme southeast corner of the county on the San Bernardino Grant. His ranch spanned both sides of the international line, but most of it was in Old Mexico—and in the direct path of the smugglers, bandits, and cattle thieves who made their headquarters in the Chihuahua Mountains, near the southern end of the San Simon Valley.

Slaughter fought his own battles against Geronimo and Apache hostiles. He was always on the alert for Indians and predatory Mexicans from south of the line who were bent on troublemaking. This rough and tortuous valley was a convenient route for outlaws from Old Mexico to northern Arizona and points beyond. It kept them away from contact with the law officers of Tombstone, Fort Huachuca, and the Territory of New Mexico.

Slaughter was not one for taking prisoners. Once, on the trail of a road agent, Slaughter caught up with the man and insisted on fighting it out. He didn't want the bother of any desperado who might, by some lucky break, turn the tables on him and kill him on the long return ride to the county jail. As soon as he learned of any murder, cattle rustling, stage holdup, or any unlawful activity, he, working alone, would take the trail. A few days later, the sheriff would return and announce he had run the outlaw clean out of the country. These killers never showed up again, either in Arizona or elsewhere.

Slaughter took no prisoners. He felt he was doing the county a service. He was saving the county court fees and the expense of keeping the outlaws locked up and fed. It also eliminated the possibility of some lawyer getting them their freedom, or of them escaping jail. Ambushed several times, he managed to escape and live a long life, dying when he was good and ready.

Some of the gun battles between law-and-order men and outlaws were unique. Constable Albert Shropshire contributed to the lore of Western gun battles when he went to arrest a Mexican man who was making trouble on Fourth Street in Duncan.

Shropshire tried to take the man without using a gun, but the villain pulled a knife on him. To save himself, he shot the man. The bullet hit the culprit in his open mouth, going through the roots of his teeth, which broke the force of the bullet.

The troublemaker insisted he swallowed the bullet. Sure enough, several days later he spit it up. It had lodged low in his throat and festered there. A coughing spell loosened the bullet. Townspeople thought that him swallowing the bullet and then spitting it out was a better story than the gun battle. That's the version they spread around Cochise County.

Not all of the lawmen were daring and courageous. Some inherited the job by default, and many of them, unfortunately, were not cut out for the life. When James Wolf first came to the Arizona Territory, a man by the name of Van Water was the constable in town. Van Water was a barber by trade, and preference. He left work early one day and entered his home only to find his wife in the arms of a lover. Van Water ran and got his rifle and pistol. When he returned, the lover took the guns away from the constable. Van Water decided to give up the job there and then and immediately left town.

Sam Starr succeeded Van Water. His jail was a deep pit in the ground with a big stake embedded in the center. He chained prisoners to the stake until he, or one of his deputies, could take them to Tombstone for incarceration in the more solid jail.

The territory had its share of bloody gunfights. Commodore Perry Owens was sheriff of Apache County when Navajo County was part of it. He was out summoning trial jury members when he rode into the livery stable in town and met Sam Brown, who warned him that the Blevins boys were in town. Owens replied that he had a warrant for the arrest of Andy Cooper (aka Andy Blevins), who was wanted in Texas. Owens told Brown that as soon as he got a bite to eat, he would go and serve the warrant. Cooper was the oldest of the Blevins Brothers and played a leading role in the Tewksbury-Graham feud (the Pleasant Valley War).

Brown told the sheriff, "Whenever you get ready to go, take plenty of help with you." Owens walked away, crossed the street, and went to the restaurant across from the railroad tracks. He returned a short time later, got his Winchester, sat down, and cleaned it carefully. He filled the magazine, put the gun under his arm, and started to walk away. On his hip he wore a six shooter and a belt full of cartridges.

Brown asked Owens where he was going, and he coolly replied, "I'm going to arrest the Blevins boys."

"Wait a minute and I'll go with you." The sheriff turned to Sam, "You stay right where you are. There is liable to be trouble. If they get me, that's all right, but I want you and everyone else to stay out of it."

Sam followed him to the front of the stable and watched as the sheriff, still carrying his Winchester under his right arm, tapped on the door with his left forefinger.

Andy Cooper came to the door, opened it a small crack, and asked Owens what he wanted. "I have a warrant for you." Cooper wanted to know what it was for, and the sheriff told him it was for stealing horses from the Navajos. Cooper replied, "I'm not going," and slammed the door in the sheriff's face.

Owens held his Winchester on his hip and fired through the door. The shot hit Cooper in the abdomen, inflicting a mortal wound. The sheriff then backed away from the door to the middle of the street.

A man by the name of Moss Roberts slipped out the back door on the north end of the house and came around on the east side with a cocked six shooter. Without raising his gun to his shoulder, Owens took a shot, killing him instantly.

In the meantime, Johnnie Blevins came out of the back door and started around the west side of the house. When he came in view, the sheriff shot him through the right shoulder. Blevins dropped his gun and fell to the ground.

Suddenly the front door was thrown open and Sam Houston Blevins, the baby of the family, a boy of fourteen, jumped out with a six shooter in his hand. His mother grabbed her baby in her arms to drag him back into the house. Owens turned his gun on the boy and shot him dead without touching the mother.

Andy Cooper lived about three hours; Johnnie recovered and served his time in the Yuma state penitentiary. After his release, he walked the straight and narrow, becoming a number one citizen.

The Blevins Ranch was in Canyon Creed, not far from Ramah. No one knew what became of the father. He went out one day to hunt horses stolen by rustlers and never returned. Years after, when the forest rangers were having some excavating done for a road, they unearthed a skeleton with a cocked gun in its hand. It bore mute evidence that someone was

Sheriff Commodore Perry Owens

quicker on the trigger and shot first. Most people thought that was what was left of Old Man Blevins.

Not everyone thought the Owens/Blevins fight was a fair one. Claude Nichols expressed the opinion of many when he said,

didn't know about the personal trouble between Commodore Owens and Andy Cooper, but from the way I heard about the killing' of the Blevins gang, I think they got about as dirty a deal from the Sheriff as any I have heard. Maybe them boys did need killing' . . . and maybe they didn't under the circumstances and the times, but Commodore Owens was the last man in the world who had any right to have killed them, even in the line of duty. But, I allow that was the only way he could ever have beaten Andy Cooper to the draw.

FIDDLING JOE

Not many women could resist Joe Hale; five foot eleven with curly black hair, he was quite handsome. However, his most striking feature were his odd eyes—devil's eyes, one looked blue, the other brown.

In 1914 Joe took it into his head that he was going to rob a bank. He shared that information with his girl in Duncan, who told him that if he did, she was through. Either he didn't believe her, or he didn't care.

After meeting his girl out on the range and announcing his plans, he took off for Duncan. Arriving at noon, he walked into the bank without any mask or disguise and with a fiddle under his arm leveled a .45 at the two employees, forcing them into the vault. One of the men pleaded for his life, saying he would surely die locked up in the vault. Hale paid no attention as he grabbed all the money in plain sight. He shut the vault, mounted his pony, and took off. In his rush he left around thirty-five thousand dollars in silver.

When Hale's girl got home that night from riding the line, she heard about the robbery. She was so upset, her family had to put her to bed. She explained her condition by telling her parents her horse threw her rather than reveal the truth.

Six months later Hale was in Texas flashing a roll of twenty-dollar crisp new bills that totaled over five hundred dollars. Officers became suspicious and started an investigation. Arrested and brought back to Arizona, he stood trial. The law convicted him of robbery, and he received a sentence of seven to twenty years in the state penitentiary.

Hale served nine years of that sentence. When the law released him, he searched out his Duncan girl, but she would have nothing to do with him. His brothers and sisters were married and didn't want Hale around their children. Hale was alone.

Hale got involved in other deviltry—bootlegging, gambling, and drinking. He got into trouble in Holbrook, and there was a bench warrant issued for his arrest. The officers knew of Hale's musical ability; when they heard fiddling coming out of a house in town, they figured they had their culprit. They looked through the window at the brightly lit room and spotted Hale, fiddling away, playing "The Prison Song," and singing at the top of his lungs.

The officers could have shot Hale right then. Instead one of them went up to the door and rapped. The lights suddenly went out, but the fiddling did not stop; it merely paused for a second. The law rushed the house, and in that instant the lights went on again. A twelve-year-old girl stood in the same spot where Joe had stood, playing the same tune on the same fiddle.

A thorough search of the premises revealed only the presence of the child and her aged grandmother, who was fussing with the light meter and muttering, "What in tarnation is the matter with the thing?" Both denied Joe Hale had been in the house.

The next thing the law heard was that Hale committed some sort of robbery in Colorado and escaped. Next news on Hale came from California. He was on the Warner Brothers radio show in Hollywood fiddling with the famous Ira Scheele.

In 1934 Hale came to Prescott, Arizona. He was no longer a hard drinker but well dressed and looking prosperous. His record with the law was clear, and he looked happy. Hale was making good money on the radio and had a contract to return to Hollywood. Perhaps he thought his newfound respectability would change his old sweetheart's mind, but her answer was the same, "I'm through." Joe left town at once.

A few days later he robbed the bank at Wilcox, alone. That put him back in the Florence prison.

WELLS FARGO HERO

The *El Paso Times* of April 25, 1895, declared, "Jeff Milton is the best Chief of Police El Paso ever had." Based on his record, Well Fargo hired Milton as a messenger and guard on the run between Benson, Arizona, and Guaymas, Mexico. It was a dangerous run, so at the same time they made him a US marshal. Milton was empowered to organize a posse to go after anyone who robbed his train.

Well Fargo carried bullion on the Benson/Guaymas route, serving a number of small gold and silver mines in the area. The position of express manager on this route carried a high risk.

Cochise County had serious problems to solve. Along with train robberies, cow rustling increased, horses disappeared, and there were more killings. It was obvious there was a vicious, well-organized gang operating in the territory, a gang that had absolute confidence in its ability to shoot its way out of any tight spot.

The bullion from the Commonwealth Mine at Pearce, and the big payrolls of Bisbee, Gleason, and Tombstone were a major attraction for holdup outlaws. Between Steins Pass and Dragoon was the most dangerous stretch. There had been several holdups of the Southern Pacific there. Pinkerton agents, railroad detectives, US marshals, and post office inspectors, plus the Cochise County sheriff's office were working on the holdups.

Then, on September 9, 1899, amid all these lawmen, the outlaws robbed the Southern Pacific of ten thousand dollars at the Cochise station. Lawmen posing as cowboys, miners, tramps, and laborers saturated the area, but came up blank. There were no clues to work with. It was a well-planned and executed robbery. The outlaws seem to know when the train would carry the most valuable cargo.

Apparently the outlaws decided to divert the attention of the lawmen from the Southern Pacific line by robbing the Wells Fargo car on the Benson-Guaymas route. Fairbanks was the place they selected for the holdup. The usual tricks of having some of the gang ride the train and cover the engineers was not going to work. The railroad was wise to these actions, and the daylight run gave them confidence. Unfortunately, for them, they selected the express car guarded by Jeff Milton.

The express car stopped directly in front of the small station to facilitate the loading of the express baggage. People crowded the platform, greeting incoming passengers and sending friends off. The crowd was large, since nearby Tombstone had no rail line.

The outlaws had to capture the messenger alive, as he alone knew the combination of the express safe. They knew Milton had courage, and was a good shot, but they also knew of his high chivalry toward women and children. The outlaws would use the women and children on the platform as a shield. They figured they could get the drop on Milton, remove his gun, clean out the safe, and make their getaway. They picked a time when the safe would be open to transfer the contents. If that didn't work, they would make Milton open it by threats or torture.

On February 15, 1900, Jess Dunlap, Bob Brown, George Owens, Lewis Owens, and John Yoes (Bravo John) drifted into Fairbanks from different directions and at different times before the arrival of the train. They gave no sign they knew each other. Each left his horse at a different handy spot near the station. Since most cowboys went around armed, their carbines caused no notice.

The small train puffed in, the express car stopped by the station, and the car's door opened. Seeing nothing suspicious, Milton began checking out his packages. The outlaws held their carbines low, the sight of them blocked by the crowd. Suddenly, from the rear of the crowd, came the shout, "Put 'em up!"

Startled, Milton looked up and immediately took in the situation—five men, five rifles, and women and children in the line of fire. Some of the crowd dropped to the ground, knowing what was coming, which left two of the outlaws exposed. The packages fell out of Milton's arms as he reached for his sawed-off shotgun with one hand and started closing the door with the other. In a lightning flash his gun went up, fatally wounding Jess Dunlap and stinging Bravo John, who spun around and left on a run. Meanwhile the other three bandits were pumping lead into Milton. He had shot the two bandits even though his left arm and shoulder were shattered.

Still shooting, the other three bandits rushed toward the car, but Milton managed to close the door and slam shut the safe before he collapsed, falling between some drummer's large sample cases.

The three remaining robbers didn't want to take any chances. Reloading their rifles, they circled the car, shooting up through the floor and through the sides. Finally satisfied that they had killed the messenger, they opened the door and discovered the safe closed and the messenger so badly shot he was useless. All the robbers got were a few Mexican pesos.

Knowing news of the holdup would be on its way to Tombstone, the three bandits loaded their wounded pal on a horse and left, heading for Wilcox and Pearce through Middlemarch in the Dragoon Mountains. Dunlap was so badly wounded he was slowing the bandits' progress, so they dumped him near the Middle Pass of the Dragoons.

Sheriff Scott White and his posse found the wounded man and brought him to Tombstone, where, before he died, he gave the authorities the names of the gang leaders. It turned out that the leaders were Wilcox Deputy Sheriff Bert Alvord and Pearce Deputy Billy Stiles. They expected the Fort Huachuca payroll to be on the train. They knew all the lawmen in town, including the disguised detectives. Ironically, they were in the front rank of the sheriff's posse on the trail of the robbers, until they were exposed as the leaders of the outlaws.

Milton hovered between life and death for months. The doctors wanted to amputate his shattered arm, but he refused. Finally Dr.

Goodfellow, from Tombstone, who was chief surgeon of the Southern Pacific Line, took charge and miraculously saved Milton's arm, though it was permanently crippled.

Milton never talked much about his colorful and dangerous life. When author Steward Edward White asked Milton about the time he and a posse chased a gang of outlaws into the mountains, Milton replied, "Why we chased that gang and caught up with them. We killed them, and they killed some of us, and that was all of that." To Milton that was the whole story.

THE DAPPER DANDY OUTLAW

Some called him Kid Joy, others said his name was King Louis, and then there were those who insisted his real name was Parson Jean de Joy. Like most outlaws, this five-foot-three, slender man with curly black hair and sloe eyes had many handles.

However, the one thing everyone agreed on was that this gunslinger was a snappy dresser.

Kid Joy distinguished himself by his clothing style. He dressed in black broadcloth suits and wore a top hat. His button shoes were accented by white spats. The white spats made him especially notable. It wasn't a fashion style often seen on the Western frontier. Kid Joy claimed to be the son of a Frenchman and a madam of a honky-tonk in New Orleans. That probably accounted for his taste in clothes.

In the early 1880s he was in Phoenix operating under the "guise" of Parson Jean de Joy. Hanging around bars and gambling rooms, he spent his time preaching to the young men who were pursuing their pleasures. One night when the poker stakes got exceptionally high, a masked bandit appeared. Armed with a pair of Colt .45s, the gunman raked in the proceeds. The most noticeable feature of the robber was his button shoes and white spats.

William T. Sanders was working in one of the Babbit brothers' line camps southwest of Flagstaff when the rider came up about dusk. "The roan hoss he was riddin was plum petered out. He had just got off with a big haul from some gambling' den round Phoenix. I gave him his supper and helped him . . . at the point of a gold-plated colt—to sort the money from the cards and poker chips. He deliberately changed horses with me and went on." It turned out Sanders made out pretty good on the exchange, as the roan turned out to be one of the finest saddle horses on the range once he was rested up.

Kid Joy's next adventure was in Navajo County, where he held up the Apache-to-Holbrook mail stage. From there he headed for Utah. Now known as King Louis, the law finally captured and convicted him for a post office robbery. The identification of the robber was easy; he wore button shoes and white spats.

Kid Joy, or King Louis, escaped from the Utah pen by what he called "the petticoat route." One Sunday afternoon a certain lady friend came with several other women to visit the prison. In those days the popular women's fashion was to wear several petticoats over a large hoop. Joy's friend brought in a bundle of woman's clothing hidden beneath her hoop. When the next group of visitors left the prison, a dainty lady left with them and departed in the waiting coach.

Kid Joy usually worked alone, however he now found himself the leader of a gang in Clifton. Some say the gang used Kid Joy to pose as the leader. Talk was that someone else issued the orders and Kid Joy passed them on. This gang rustled stock and forced people to buy the beef. Reluctant customers were assaulted in alleyways or robbed and beaten in their stores.

Word came to James Colquhoun, who worked for the mining company, that King Louis's gang was targeting the company's warehouse where they kept the bullion and gold dust. The plan was to rob the warehouse and kidnap Colquhoun. The day the robbery was planned, the gang rustled some fine saddle horses from the stables of two Mexicans in Little San Francisco. The afternoon of the planned robbery, Kid Joy, in a jealous rage, shot a woman called Little Nell, who lived in Chase Creek. Little Nell supposedly was the woman who helped him escape in Utah.

Remorseful, he sent for the doctor in an attempt to save Little Nell, but the doctor failed to arrive in time and the woman died in the outlaw's arms. Fueled with white-hot rage, the King went gunning for the doctor, who went into hiding in the home of a friend. Although they searched the town, the gang never discovered the doctor. The next day they waylaid a stagecoach, thinking the doctor might be trying to get out of town.

Meanwhile the enraged Mexicans, who lost their saddle horses, had organized a vigilante committee and went hunting for the thieving gang. As they rode around a bend in Ward's Canyon, they came face-to-face with the Joy gang. The gang members rapidly scattered, leaving Kid Joy alone to face the enraged Mexicans. Filled with bravado, the outlaw rode straight into the fusillade. When they picked up the body of Kid Joy, they found him riddled with bullets. He was dressed in black broadcloth, a silk top hat, patent leather button shoes, and white spats.

A WEAKNESS FOR WOMEN

Lee Woods, or Lee Wright, was one of the homeliest men you could find. He was over six feet tall and had a lanky raw-bone frame, small black eyes, black hair, and a long pointed nose that looked more like a beak. Yet, despite his unattractiveness, all the women fell for Woods and he fell for beautiful women—as many as possible. His name was Lee Woods, but sometime in his lawless career, he changed it to Wright.

Wright rustled cattle in Arizona, running them across the border where he sold them to a fence called Pedro Garcia. He was never known as a holdup man, but he could skin the lining out of your pockets in a poker game, and was quick on the draw.

The outlaw met young Ellen Wright in one of the honky-tonks in Tombstone. He took her to his hideout in Cave Creek and made her cook for his gang over the campfire. Ellen wasn't much of a cook, but the gang pretended to like it.

When Tombstone's Sheriff Earp made life uncomfortable for Wright and his gang, the outlaw figured it was time to go. He and Ellen left the area, and his gang scattered. A year later Ellen and Wright were married in El Paso under the name Woods. They were at Lee's mother's house in San Antonio when the law caught up to them and arrested Wright on an old murder charge. He spent the next years in the Texas penitentiary, leaving Ellen with his mother.

When Wright got out of jail, he returned to San Antonio and remarried Ellen, this time using the name of Wright. It was a grand affair conducted in the Methodist church with carefully selected guests. Even though Wright's best man was a prison pal, the affair was as fine as the most sophisticated big city weddings.

Ellen's wedding dress was made of pure white satin and trimmed with seed pearls and point lace. She had six bridesmaids. Her bridegroom knew all but one. He met Annie Barnes, a petite brunet on the day of the wedding. Ellen had a few bad moments, fearful that her bridegroom would elope with Annie before their wedding. Lee just settled on dancing with the pretty Annie all night, allowing his new bride only one dance.

The next morning the Wrights and their best man, Bill Cook, headed south for their honeymoon in a covered wagon. In Juarez, Mexico, Wright got too friendly with an entertainer in the Black Cat Cafe and wound up in a shoot-out with her man. Wright killed the lover, who turned out to be a very popular bullfighter. The Wrights and Cook left town in a hurry. They had worn out their welcome out in Juarez.

The three arrived in Columbus, New Mexico and decided to go to Clifton, Arizona. On route the Wrights changed their mind and decided to head for Duncan, but Cook continued on to Clifton.

The Wrights homesteaded in Parke Canyon, and Lee opened a blacksmith shop called the Tong Shop. In 1910 he took in a partner by the name of J. H. Gooch. It looked like the Wrights had settled down and become good citizens.

However, old habits don't die, and it wasn't long before Lee was involved with other women. Ellen was insanely jealous of her husband and his roving eye. She would fly into a rage at the mere mention of another woman's name. Of course she had reason for her jealousy. The arguments always went the same way. Ellen would accuse her husband, they would fight, and in a rage, he would beat her. Regretting the beatings, he would buy Ellen a peace offering, such as an expensive gown or a piece of jewelry. Ellen wore the finest gowns and the biggest diamonds of any woman in the Duncan valley, and she carried the blackest eyes.

An entertainer on Chase Creek in Clifton caught Wright's attention. She was a beautiful woman, but not as lovely as his wife, black eyes or no. Wright's trips to Clifton became more frequent, and Ellen's eyes never healed. Then he gave her such a bad beating, the doctor was called.

Sheriff Charlie Sands sent Wright word he was going to arrest him for wife beating. Wright went downtown, unarmed, and met with the sheriff. They met on Main Street in front of Wright's shop, The Tong Shop. "Put up your hands, you are under arrest," announced Sands, leveling his Colt 45 straight at Lee. Wright didn't smile, and he didn't put up his hands. "Put that damn thing away fore I make yeh eat the sight offen' it," drawled Wright.

While Sands was no coward, he had no desire to kill Wright and knew that if he insisted on the arrest, he'd have to shoot it out. He had no idea Wright was unarmed.

"If you can't get along with that little woman without beating her half to death, you ought to leave her."

Wright didn't answer. He gave the sheriff a stony stare, then turned and went into The Tong Shop. He sold his interest in the shop to his partner. He left town that evening, leaving his wife the homestead and every dollar he had, which was a neat nest egg. Wright divorced Ellen as quickly as possible and married again. However, his new wife was not the girl in Clifton.

In 1916, Wright killed a man at the fairgrounds in Phoenix. The circumstances are unknown, but shortly after that he became a peace officer. Apparently Wright had seen the error of his ways and immediately reformed.

On January 20, 1920, events unfolding in Pennsylvania were to have drastic consequences in far-off Arizona. Irene Schroeder, with her brother Tom Crawford and her lover Glen Dague, killed Corporal Brady Paul, a patrol officer on a highway near Newcastle, Pennsylvania. They made their getaway in a stolen Chrysler roadster and continued their flight westward through Missouri, Oklahoma, Texas, and New Mexico, eventually entering Arizona. Somewhere along the route, Crawford left them.

Crawford and an associate committed a robbery in Caruthersville, Missouri, and were hunted down, but they managed to survive a gunfight. The law caught up with Crawford at Cape Girardeau, Missouri, and killed him; his partner was wounded, captured, and sent to prison for life.

Now somewhere in Texas, the Schroeder gang picked up Joe F. Wells, a convict recently released from the Texas penitentiary. They headed into

Arizona. When they reached Florence, Dague and Wells got out of the car, and Schroeder drove into a service station. Laying on a hard-luck story about a sick mother in Yuma and not having any money, she was able to obtain three gallons of gas. She was the perfect picture of a beautiful woman in distress. She drove to another gas station. This time her story was about her very sick child in Yuma. However, this gas station attendant did not fall for her sad story.

Deputy Sheriff Joe Chapman came into the station at this time, and suspecting foul play, asked Schroeder to produce the title to her car. Realizing she was in a tight spot, she signaled her companions by blasting on her horn. Guns in hand, they ran across the street and grabbed Chapman. They robbed the deputy of the ten dollars in his pocket, took his watch, handcuffed him with his own cuffs, and shoved him into the car between Dague and Schroeder, who held a gun against his ribs as they drove away.

Driving in unfamiliar territory, the gang forced directions from Chapman. He sent them in a circuitous route, hoping to gain time for the law to catch up with them. Attempting to cross the Gila River, the car mired down, and the gangsters removed Chapman's handcuffs so he could help push the car out of the muck. He then directed them to Chandler, telling them there was less chance of officers being in that location. Although he knew that is where the law was waiting.

In Chandler, Shirley Butterfield and Lee Wright were waiting in Butterfield's car. They sat at the junction of the plaza and the road south to Casa Grande with the engine running, watching for the roadster. Sheriff Walter Laveen of Pinal County had sent out an alert on Chapman's kidnapping.

Butterfield and Wright spotted the car as it entered the plaza, not doing more than twenty miles an hour. Butterfield blew sharp blasts on the horn, signaling the car to stop. The gangsters ignored the signal. Butterfield drew abreast of the smaller vehicle and forced it to the curb, angling his vehicle in front of the roadster. A man riding in the rumble seat of the roadster opened fire. Butterfield and Wright returned fire, Butterfield with a revolver and Wright with a shotgun.

As the cars came to a stop, Chapman seized the right hands of the man and woman next to him in the car in an effort to keep them from firing.

At the same time, he kicked the car door open just as the first charge from Wright's shotgun struck the occupants of the vehicle. Chapman received a hail of buckshot in his extended hands. Struck by bullets, he rolled out of the car to the ground. He tried to drag the woman with him, but failed.

The gangsters got Wright in the shoulder, severing a blood vessel. Splintered glass from his windshield left bleeding cuts on Butterfield's face and hands. Seeing citizens rushing over to offer aid, the gunmen backed their car out of the stopped position and fled.

The alarm went out. Bridges were guarded, all cars stopped and searched. The bandits took the mountain route, reaching South Mountain Park; they wandered around most of the night, finally emerging on Southern Avenue. They mistakenly thought this was the road to Yuma. After driving several miles, the paved road turned to dirt. That's when they saw the lights of three cars—one behind them, two in front.

Believing officers hemmed them in, they pulled off to the side of the road. Under cover of darkness they abandoned the car and struck out across the fields and desert. They traveled about twelve miles, wading across the Gila River eight miles south and west of Laveen.

Because of the recent rains, they left a trail that was easy to track. They made it into the mountains and fortified themselves, prepared to give battle. The odds were not on their side, 3 against 110 officers of the law who were well armed and had plenty of ammunition.

The gangsters' ammunition got low, the desert sun was beating them down, and they had no water and had not had anything to eat since the day before. Late that day, realizing their situation was hopeless, they surrendered.

Irene Schroeder and her lover, Glen Dague, were surrendered to the Pennsylvania authorities, where they went to trial, were found guilty of the murder of Corporal Brady Paul, and executed in the electric chair. Lee Wright, seriously wounded, died in the Mesa hospital. He lived for beautiful women, and he died by the hand of the most beautiful of them all.

BAD SCOUT, GOOD SCOUT

During the heavy Indian warfare years from 1875 to 1886, Al Sieber, chief Arizona scout adopted the son of Apache Chief Togo-do-chus. He called the boy Apache Kid, sent him to school, and later made him a scout, eventually promoting him to first sergeant.

The trouble all started for the Apache Kid when Old Rip killed his father at an Indian dance. According to the Apache code of honor, it was up to the Apache Kid to revenge his father's death by killing his murderer. Al Sieber warned him not to harm Old Rip. The Kid listened but said nothing.

Sieber and Captain Pierce, the agent at the San Carlos Reservation, headed up to Fort Apache leaving the Kid in charge of the scouts at the agency. As soon as they left, the Apache Kid took five of his men and went up to the camp of Old Rip and shot him. After the killing, they headed for the Kid's tribe.

When Sieber returned, he ordered the Apache Kid to come into the agency. The Apache Kid showed up with eleven of his warriors. Sieber drew a line in front of his tent and then told the Apache Kid to take the guns and cartridge belts from the five who had government rifles. He ordered Kid Apache to take his belt and lay it on the ground with his rifle. Again, the Apache Kid complied. Next, he ordered the six men to go to the guardhouse. Some of the Indians resisted, and Sieber, setting his rifle, shot one of them. All hell broke loose, and in the ensuing gunfight the Indians wounded Sieber in his weak leg and escaped. The Apaches, led by the Apache Kid, went on the warpath and committed several murders before the army troops were able to run them down and capture the Apache Kid.

In 1889 in Globe, Arizona, during the fall term of the US District Court, the Apache Kid was convicted of desertion and sentenced to a long term in prison. However, after serving a short time, President Grover Cleveland pardoned him. Immediately after his release, he was arrested by the civil authorities of Gila County and charged with murder. In July 1890 the Apache Kid and five of his companions received a sentence of life imprisonment at Yuma.

A small posse, made up of Sheriff Glen Reynolds, special deputy William Holmes, the driver Eugene Middleton, and a member of a Tonto Basin family who was having trouble with the Apaches, was transporting thirty-five Indians and one Mexican prisoner in a special stage. The route took them over the Pinal Mountains on the way to the Yuma penitentiary. On the second day of the journey, on the Gila River near the town of Kelvin, the sheriff took six of the shackled prisoners from the stage, which was at the bottom of a steep sand wash. As the party trudged up the hill, two of the Indians suddenly grabbed the sheriff and two others reeled around on Holmes. Holmes fell backward as his pistol was wrenched from his hand. They shot Sheriff Reynolds and then turned and shot Holmes through the heart.

Middleton was in the stage at the bottom of the wash, guarding the remaining two prisoners. One of them was the Apache Kid, who shouted, "I will sit down, don't shoot." The stage position made it impossible to see what was going on with the others up the bank, and Middleton assumed the shots came from the sheriff. Moments later the Mexican, seeking shelter, ran up just as one of the escaped Indians, using the sheriff's rifle, fired from behind the coach at Middleton.

The four horses bolted. Middleton fell to the ground, shot through the cheek, neck, and left side of his body. The Indians rolled him over searching for valuables. He felt the cold muzzle of a rifle against his temple when he heard the Apache Kid say, "Save the cartridges, he is dead anyhow." The Mexican prisoner escaped and made his way back to Florence to report the incident. For this, the governor later pardoned him.

Leaving Middleton still "playing possum," the Indians unshackled themselves, took the commitment papers from the dead sheriff's pocket, tore them up, and left the scene. Middleton waited until he felt it was safe to move. Horribly wounded, he staggered to his feet. Looking at Holmes's body, he saw it was untouched, but the gun muzzle had cut his face and his forehead had been smashed with a rock.

It took Middleton the rest of that day and the night to travel the five miles back to the Riverside station. A posse from Globe started on the trail of the fugitives, but had to return when a snowstorm hit.

The renegade Indians had gone up the river to the mouth of the San Pedro near the site of the town of Hayden, and then on to the San Carlos reservation. Indian scouts at San Carlos killed most of the outlaw Indians. They tried, convicted, and sentenced to life imprisonment at Yuma one of the outlaw Indians, who was wounded in the escape attempt.

The Apache Kid escaped and took out his revenge from the Tonto Basin to the Sierra Madre Mountains of Mexico. There were a number of murders in the area, and everyone suspected the Apache Kid had committed them all, even though there was no evidence. He returned to the San Carlos reservation several times. A few times, he stole squaws, but fear kept the Indians from reporting his visits until after he left.

From time to time, the Apache Kid would gather small bands of outlaw Apaches and attack his targets in force. One such occasion, on December 12, 1890, renegade Indians surrounded Gun Hinkey, Jack Bridger, and Buck Robinson on a hillside twenty miles southeast of the San Bernardino ranch. Hinkey was there to see a steer believed killed by a band of Indians led by the Apache Kid. When the three arrived at the steer, one of the cowboys swiftly raised his rifle and shot an Indian, who happened to be on his way back for more beef. That was when the men realized that they stumbled onto a band of twelve Indians. One of them was Big Foot, whose moccasin track shoe was fourteen inches long.

The cowboys took refuge behind the rocks. They were beginning to feel secure, when a shot knocked a corncob pipe from Hinkey's mouth. Bridger thought that was funny, and laughing, he leaned forward, taking a shot to the head. A few minutes later, another shot killed Robinson. Hinkey took off running, outracing an Apache. He struck the trail for camp along the bottom of a sandy gorge with some flowing water. Jumping behind a boulder on the side of the canyon, he took off at a right angle; the Indians kept running down the canyon on the well-trodden trail. Hinkey, cut off from his horse, headed for the Milt Hall ranch on foot, fourteen miles away.

When men arrived at the massacre the next day, they found the bodies had not been mutilated, but the heads had been crushed by rocks. There was no sign of the Indians, no sign of the Apache Kid.

In 1899, Colonel Kosterlitzsky, a Mexican official, declared that the Apache Kid was still alive and was the head of a little settlement of well-behaved Apaches living in the Sierra Madre Mountains in Mexico.

The man tied mostly to the Apache Kid, was Al Sieber, chief army scout. While the Apache Kid is known for having been an army scout turned bad, Sieber is reputed to have been the best scout the army ever had. His exploits are legendary.

It was in a lonesome valley in the Sierra Madres Mountains, far from the US border that Sieber, along with his Apache scouts, a small band of soldiers, and General George Crook, were having one of their most important and dangerous meetings. They were in this isolated valley to meet with Geronimo.

Sieber found his party surrounded, and outnumbered, by hostile Apaches. He turned to scout Tom Horn. Selecting him as the interpreter, he pushed him forward with these instructions: "Take a knife, Tom. Stand while you interpret. Forget that you may not live another minute and think only of the talk."

The Apaches had agreed to this conference, but no one in the army group knew if it was to talk terms, to surrender, to stall, or to kill the army representatives. Sieber took no chances and kept his hand in his shirt on his revolver. He intended to blow Geronimo's brains out at the first hostile move. He honed his nerves of steel during the twenty-one years he served as an Indian scout for the army under Generals Stoneman, Miles, Kratz, Wilcox, Guerson, and Crook. If ever there was a man who knew no fear, it was Al Sieber. He was an imposing man, six foot one and 190 pounds of muscle and confidence. He earned that confidence at Gettysburg, where he fought on the Union side. He also earned a severe gunshot wound that left him with a weak leg and a limp.

Sieber arrived in Arizona's Williamson Valley in 1869 to take up farming. The area was having serious problems with the Apaches, whom the soldiers seemed unable to control. The citizens of Williamson Valley decided to fight back; they organized and appointed Sieber as their leader. Sieber was able to recover some of the stolen stock and in the process managed to kill many of the hostiles.

The army noticed his success and offered him a position as an army scout. Initially he served as a scout operating out of Camp Huachuca. His acquaintance with the Apache ways made him an especially valuable man in leading the scouts.

Throughout his scouting career Sieber was in constant danger and bore twenty-nine wounds from Indian fights. Many of the Indians held personal grudges against him, yet he went about his work as though everyone in the entire world was his friend.

Although Sieber treated his scouts with respect, he thought nothing of going into a camp of crazed Apaches at Fort Apache, kick, and slap them about as if they were children. Not one of them ever resisted or showed any resentment. He could control a bunch of Apaches where mutiny was brewing and it wasn't safe for anyone else to try.

Sieber's own associates say he was always self-possessed and dignified with the scouts. He believed it was his duty to deal with these Apaches. He trained them and expected loyalty from them. In case of disloyalty on a scouting trip, the punishment was immediate. He would shoot them in front of their companions.

Although he could talk good Apache, he never gave an order of any importance to a scout without an interpreter. Once he was asked, "Why do you send for an interpreter when you can talk as well as he can?" He replied, "I do not want any come back. There has been grave mistakes made and I do not want a repetition."

Al Williamson, a packer for Sieber, recalled his tough ways. On one scouting trip, they were gone for weeks and were able to capture a big buck Indian. The orders from headquarters were to "bring in no prisoners." Yet Sieber kept this buck with him for several days, thinking that perhaps he could get something out of him concerning the location of the renegades. They were nearing camp and all of Sieber's men were aware of the orders and wondered what he would do. The Indian scouts there either didn't understand, or didn't want to understand.

Everyone was sitting around a circle eating breakfast with the packer sitting next to the Indian. Sieber took his Winchester rifle, put it right in back of the Indian's head, and shot him behind the ear just as he was biting into a piece of bread. He flipped over backward; his feet went straight up in the air. The annoyed packer turned to Sieber and said, "Al, if I had known you were going to do that to him I would not have let him eat so much."

Another scouting trip took Sieber above Payson, where renegades had been committing depredations. Sieber sent some scouts ahead to locate them. The scouts spotted the Indians' Rancheria up on a ridge. When they reported to Sieber, he took his main body of scouts and headed out that night. They left their horses at the foot of the ridge and started up the slope on foot. By then it was snowing very hard and they wanted to get to the top by daylight. They plowed five miles through the snowstorm and reached their destination about an hour before dawn.

Sieber and his scouts kept circling around the trees, trying to keep warm by walking. When it was light enough to see, they attacked. It had been such a stormy night that the renegades had posted no guards, supposing no one would follow them in such weather. The scouts wiped out the Rancheria, killing men, women, and children. No scouts were lost, but the mother of one of the scouts, who was with the renegades, was dead. They had to lay over for two days so the scout could mourn for his mother.

In 1882, Geronimo's renegades were making devastating raids from their camp in the Sierra Madres in Mexico into settlements in the United States. Sieber and scout Tom Horn struck the trail and ran upon them at Hot Springs, Mexico. Sieber shot a warrior, and Tom captured the dead warrior's squaw. They turned the woman over to the soldiers in Fort Rucker, saying they had found her and the warrior at the head of Guadalupe Canyon in Arizona—an important location, as the Mexican Government prohibited forays into their country.

The Mexicans found the dead warrior on their side of the border. Following the trail, they noted that it led back into the United States. The Mexican Government protested over the invasion. At San Carlos the Indian woman testified she was at Hot Springs, Mexico, when captured. Al Sieber and Tom Horn were in trouble. The War Department investigated the matter and ordered Sieber and Horn reprimanded. At the army post, an officer received orders to handle the situation. He called the head scouts in and explained the whole business. Having fulfilled his duty, he invited them to dinner and a drink.

By early 1883, trouble with the Apaches took a more serious and desperate turn. However, the US Government now had an agreement with the Mexican Government allowing American soldiers to cross the border into Mexico in pursuit of the Apaches. General Crook was in command of this mission.

Sieber and Horn took the woman they had captured and turned her loose with orders to tell Geronimo that the American soldiers wanted to talk with him. Geronimo got the message and agreed to a conference.

Scout Tom Horn
COURTESY LEGENDS OF AMERICA

On this Geronimo expedition to Mexico with Sieber, Crook enlisted five companies of Indian scouts to hunt the Apaches. A company usually consisted of twenty-six privates, two sergeants, and two corporals. However, in this expedition the companies of enlisted men were much larger. Sergeants and corporals were selected from the chiefs and other leading men in the tribe. To avoid problems among the Indian scouts, the army tried to keep members of the same tribe together. They chose Mickey Free as the interpreter on this expedition. He held the rank of first sergeant.

Seven scouts made up a secret-service force. It was dangerous duty assigned only to the most discreet and trustworthy Indians on the reservation. Two of the seven were women. The spies had no part in the military expeditions; their duty was to note and report secretly to Army Lieutenants Crawford and Gatewood any sign of mutiny, hostility, or unrest among the Indians.

Sieber's last official military position was as chief of scouts on the San Carlos reservation. This was probably the most dangerous position ever filled by a white man in the Southwest. While at San Carlos, a recalcitrant Indian scout shot him. At the time, Sieber was attempting to disarm a threatening band of Indians. That shot seriously crippled him and incapacitated him for further active service. His scouting days were over.

After Sieber's scouting career ended, his next job for the government was at the Roosevelt Dam building site. He was the foreman of a large gang of Apache Indians employed in constructing a road.

A boulder weighing about thirty tons was blocking the trail. Understanding the dangerousness of the location, Sieber sent all but one Indian ahead. His plan was to cut enough earth out so he could stick a piece of dynamite under the rock. As he was pushing under the rock, he saw it move and yelled for the Indian worker to get out of the way. The boulder toppled on Sieber, crushing him from his stomach down. He never regained consciousness.

They buried Al Sieber, chief of scouts, in the Globe cemetery. They marked his grave with a monument erected by the Territory of Arizona.

A LIFE OF JUSTICE

James Parks knew the outlaws of his time, having dealt with most of them in one way or another, as

Scout and outlaw The Apache Kid
COURTESY OF LEGENDS OF AMERICA

a cowboy, deputy, sheriff, and US marshal. He wore his first law badge in 1888 when he was twenty-one years old, and he carried an officer's commission his whole life. During that time, he crossed paths with such desperados as the Apache Kid, Billy Grounds, Three-Fingered Black Jack Ketchum, and Lee Wright. He served as a deputy under Pop Anderson in Graham County, and eventually served two terms as sheriff of that county.

Things were still rough and dangerous as the century turned, and in 1906, as he remembered it, he was in Clifton when a pair of Texas Rangers arrived looking for train robbers. The rangers were working on a tip that the outlaws were out at the Double Circle Ranch. A posse including the sheriff, rangers, and Parks headed out to the ranch.

The posse arrived at sundown and found the suspected train robbers, the Bedford boys, busting broncos in the corral. One of them was unarmed, which made it slightly easier to take them in, but the posse didn't get off without bloodshed.

No one knows who started the gunfight or whose bullets did the killings. When the shooting started, Bood Brookin and two of his men rushed out of the house and started firing at the two men in the corral. Brookin didn't want anyone to think he was willingly harboring outlaws.

They got the outlaws, buried them right on the ranch, and didn't take time to make coffins. The law had two of their own dead, and one wounded man to be cared for.

Talk was that the robbers had the train robbery loot with them. Brookin denied any knowledge of the money. Three months later the Bell Brothers, who were helping with round up at the Double Circle when the robbers were there, were found shot to death at Eagle Creek. They were riddled with bullets, but the law had no clues as to who had shot them or why.

Parks became sheriff of Graham County in 1901, a position he held until 1909 when he received a US marshal's commission. One of the toughest men he had to face was Augestine Cahone. Cahone killed Pablo Salcedo in Morenci, Arizona. He was tried and the verdict was hanging. He broke out of the Solomonville jail, and Parks initiated a manhunt that covered from Solomonville to the Mexican border. On the run, Cahone killed a Mexican horse wrangler at the Horseshoe Ranch, near the New Mexico line, and stole a fresh mount there. At the Cave Creek Ranch, toward Douglas, he killed another man and stole supplies and a horse.

Bert Alvord, Parks's undersheriff, gathered a posse of fifty men and went in one direction. Parks headed in another direction, and Captain Mossman and his troop spread out from Fort Grant. Mossman captured Cahone at Naco. The army met Parks at Benson and turned the prisoner over to the sheriff, who slammed him back in jail. They built the scaffold right in the courtyard; Cahone could see the scaffold going up from his cell. He watched but showed no emotion. It was as if he was seeing a chicken coop being erected.

According to the law, the prisoner had one last request. Cahone asked for a pot of coffee made over a campfire. John Eppley, the official hangman, made the coffee, but Cahone refused to drink it, saying, "Better let the sheriff and his brave posse drink that coffee, they need it to brace them up to get nerve to pull that rope." Hearing that, Eppley refused to pull the rope. That pleased the sheriff, who was anxious to do it himself and get it over. Parks pulled the rope with real relish and honestly wished Cahone had about a dozen necks to break.

More trouble came Parks way in 1901 when Fillipe Ortego killed two miners at Morenci. The sheriff found the two bodies floating in the leaching pond several days after they were reported missing. The miners' cabin had been robbed of everything of value, and there was blood on the floor. The law found a few fingerprints, but no other clues.

Parks heard rumors that Fillipe Ortego and his friends and relatives went on a drinking spree, left their jobs, and went fishing on Eagle Creek. There was a high-stakes poker game in the miners' cabin on payday three days before the discovery of the bodies.

Parks went out with only one deputy to find Ortego. The two of them brought in twelve outlaws, handcuffed together, and drove them like a bunch of sheep to the jail in Clifton.

Ortego confessed to the murder, claimed he did it by himself. He said he robbed them after they had won all his and his friends' money in the poker game. Ortego got the death sentence, and Parks took him to Solomonville for the hanging. He was handcuffed to his saddle and tied to his horse. Parks connected his saddle to Ortego's with a chain. They slipped out at night to avoid any mobs bent on hanging Ortego.

Ortego told Parks his friends had started the rumors of a mob to get him to leave at night. They were waiting for the sheriff, the prisoner told him, and they were going to take him away from Parks. Sure enough, as they were crossing a dry wash, a few miles from the Clifton cutoff, a gang of Mexicans surrounded the sheriff. "Reach," they ordered, and he did, with his pistols in each hand. Parks's first shot got Ortego. When the rescuers saw Ortego slumped in the saddle, they took off, shooting back at Parks as they ran. They managed to nick the sheriff's shoulder and put a crease in his head.

Parks emptied his guns at the fleeing Mexicans and reached for his rifle when he heard shooting coming from about three hundred yards down the road. He dismounted and ducked behind a rock ready to fight, and then he spied two of his deputies coming up the trail. They decided to follow him, just in case of trouble. Two Mexicans died along with Ortego. The deputies dug a grave in the sand wash and buried all three outlaws there.

Tough Town

The citizens of Duncan kept Parks and all their future lawmen busy. There was the incident with the old prospector who liked to come into town and go on a drinking spree. One night, in 1914, he came in and showed a huge bankroll. Then he got sloppy drunk and fell asleep in an alley. That was too easy for some of the town's villains. Four or five young men, between the ages of fourteen and seventeen, rolled the old man. They got his cash, and Earl Sands, who was the law then, got them. The big roll of money turned out to be two one-dollar bills wrapped around a corncob. The "drunken" old man stood outside the jail laughing his fool head off. He not only didn't have a roll of money, he wasn't even drunk. The boys couldn't pay their fines, so they spent sixty days in jail. They turned out to be model citizens after that.

Duncan remained a wild town long into the thirties. It was such a tough town that the wife of the justice of the peace beat him up and had him arrested every so often. The town had three saloons and two other places to buy whiskey. On a festive night, things happened. Down by the Bonnie Heather Saloon, a drunken woman knocked Bent Layton off his stool and dared him to hit her. He didn't, but the sheriff hauled them both off to jail to sober up.

Meanwhile, behind the Duncan Mercantile, Stanley Coon, the manager, was sitting in the backyard cooling off when a man slipped behind him and tied a piece of wire around his neck. He ordered the manager to open the safe. When the manager explained they would have to go to the front of the store, as the back door was barred, the robber decided to settle for what was in Coon's pockets. Coon gave him two dollars, then, as he was reaching into his pocket for his billfold with thirty dollars, the thief got scared and took off. His only reward for his outlaw ways was the two dollars.

A Mysterious End

It was in the late 1800s that A. M. Franklin met John Ringo. Fortunately, it turned out to be more of a business deal than a life-threatening situation. Franklin's mission was to receive a herd of about a thousand head of cattle at San Simon Station. The point he selected to bed down the cattle was in the center of the valley. It gave the wranglers a broad outlook toward the Mexican line and over to the Galeyville country, where, as Franklin recalls, a number of cowboys and rustlers made their rendezvous and business headquarters.

The cattle reached the valley about four thirty in the afternoon, and the men drew straws for the watches. Franklin, Jim Sprague, and four Mexican herders got the first watch, which ended at midnight. As the watch ended, Sprague began unsaddling. Suddenly there was considerable noise and a commotion disturbed the night and frightened the cattle. As soon as the stampede started, Franklin mounted his still-saddled horse and took off. Since the cattle were heading toward him, he rode hell-bent for leather to get out of the way. The faster he went, the faster the cattle kept after him. One of the wranglers, Joe Browning, mounted on a fast horse, was madly waving his red handkerchief trying to get Franklin's attention.

Browning finally caught up to Franklin, "You damn fool, haven't you got sense enough to circle around so as to get the cattle milling and stop this damn stampede? You've been the ringleader of it for the last four miles."

After an hour they were able to stop the cattle and hold them steady. The first watch now bedded down, the second watch took over. The next morning Franklin sent the two Mexican herders back to the first camp to cut signs east, north, and west. In about four hours the herders returned and reported that it looked as if 150 to 200 head of cattle had gone toward Galeyville. They found signs of five or six different shod horses.

John Ringo had cut out the 150 to 200 from the stampeding herd. Sprague was missing, and that meant he, not Franklin, had started the stampede. Franklin saddled up and followed the tracks, which led to the lower foothills of Galeyville. As Franklin followed the trail, he spotted small groups of cattle. And he was sure they were his cattle, because the herd was all black, and so were these bunches.

Arriving in Galeyville, Franklin went into a saloon without a name and the first person he saw was John Ringo, who said, "What the hell are you doing up here?" Franklin tossed a twenty-dollar gold piece on the bar and said he was buying drinks for the whole house and would keep buying until the money was gone. There were seven other cowboys or rustlers besides Ringo in the room.

After the fifth round, Ringo wanted to know why Franklin was there. He answered that he had had a bit of bad luck with a bunch of steers, they stampeded, and he was about 175 head short. Ringo wanted to know if he had seen anything coming up the trail. Franklin told him, "I thought I did but I'm not sure."

Ringo was born and raised in Texas, near the border, and there was no love between him and Mexicans. He couldn't hide his disappointment as he replied, "Why in hell didn't you send your Mexicans up to get your cattle?" Ringo had made it clear that he would rather shoot a Mexican than a rattlesnake.

Franklin got down to business. "If you and your fellows will round up the cattle I've lost and deliver them to me at the San Carlos Apache Indian Reservation it will be worth ten dollars a head, or it will be worth five dollars a head to me if you can deliver them to me at San Jose." That was the first settlement on the Gila River after it left the mountains.

Ringo wanted to know how much money Franklin had. "A little over a hundred dollars, enough to carry me to San Carlos, at which point I can get all the money I want," was the answer.

"Well," the outlaw said, "give me a hundred and I'll see what the boys and myself can do about the round up." Franklin handed over the hundred, and before they arrived at San Jose, the steers were delivered.

John Ringo first made his Arizona presence known in Tombstone in 1881. He immediately sought out the roughest kind. In the next years, he had headquarters at Charleston, Galeyville, the old Hughes Ranch in Cochise County, and a few places in Sonora, Mexico.

He was over six feet tall, rangy, bony, and strong. His eyes were light blue, and he had an innocent, sweet air. You couldn't help liking him, but when he was drunk you wanted to avoid him at all costs. He was the best pistol shot in the country. His favorite trick was to hold a Colt .45 on the index finger of each hand, barrels down, and at a signal give them a three-quarter turn while shooting both at beer bottles. He could the hit the bottles' neck two out of three times at fifty feet.

Ringo had a gang of six to eight, the number increasing or decreasing depending on the conditions. They were all young, and their occupation was to steal horses from one place, drive them to another, and sell them for a third of their market value. Possession was nine tenths of the law then, no bills of sale. If the owner caught up to them, he would have to pay the going rate to get them back.

When the Law and Order League of Tombstone decided to conduct a "clean-up" and put an end to the outlaws, the capture of John Ringo and his lieutenant Curley Bill was their first consideration. The league posse, consisting of fifty men all heavily armed with shotguns, left for Charleston. As they reached one end of the bridge across the San Pedro, Ringo, also heavily armed, reached the opposite end. Ringo spoke six words: "Come on. I'm waiting for you." The Law and Order League stopped, then turned toward Tombstone, and hurried home.

Ringo was an avid poker player and didn't much appreciate losing. At the Evilsizer's Saloon in Galeyville he watched a fellow player spread down four aces. Ringo drew and calmly remarked, "A six shooter beats four aces." Then he pocketed the five-hundred-dollar pot and rode away.

A week later Ringo was arrested by Deputy Breakenridge for armed robbery. He had some business matters to take care of, so he bargained with the deputy. "Tell you how we'll fix it up, Billy. You hit the trail and as soon as I've straighten up my affairs I'll catch up with you. You have John Ringo's word." The next morning John Ringo showed up keeping his promise to Deputy Breakenridge.

As a boy Henry Smith and his family knew John Ringo. He was viewed as a brave, smart, well-educated, and courteous man. His most outstanding characteristic seems to have been his absolute truthfulness. Ringo prided himself on keeping his word.

Ringo's death is a puzzle yet to be definitely solved. Smith lived where they found the outlaw's body, and he was positive Ringo was murdered. Ringo had been on a drunken spree with Billy Claiborne and Frank Leslie. They went from saloon to saloon, starting in Tombstone, on to Soldier Holes and Patterson's. From Patterson's Ringo went off alone, saying

Outlaw John Ringo

he was going to Galeyville. Bill Sanders met Ringo on the trail, but they didn't speak. Several miles later Sanders met Frank Leslie. Leslie wanted to know if Ringo had passed that way, and when told he had, he hurried on to overtake him.

Near the Smith place there was a stone seat built into a large live oak tree on the bank of the creek. In this seat Ringo was found dead the next day by Jim Morgan. Mrs. Smith heard the shot about noon the previous day and thought her brother, Will, had killed a deer. Will heard the shot and, fearing an Indian attack, hurriedly headed for home. The shot puzzled everyone, but then they thought perhaps it was a neighbor hunting.

Ringo had his six shooter in his right hand. The gun had apparently fallen as he shot, catching in his watch chain. The watch was still running. Smith believes Ringo was shot and the gun placed to look like suicide. There were no powder marks of any kind on his hands or his body. Billy Claiborne said on his deathbed that Leslie murdered Ringo and that he was an eyewitness to the murder. Leslie was a man who killed for the thrill of it. Some even heard Leslie boast that he "got" John Ringo. Ringo was buried where he died, his grave covered with rocks.

CHAPTER 2

Miners and Prospectors

Gold is where you find it.

—HENRY WICKENBURG

A few men might leave home for a pretty face, but the promise of riches can start a migration. The news of the discovery of gold at Sutter's Mill, California, in 1848 rang around the world like a siren's song. Over three hundred thousand gold seekers arrived in the Southwest looking for riches. At least half of them followed the California and Gila River Trails, which took them through the land that would become part of the Arizona Territory.

Many of the California gold seekers found their way back to Arizona when their western-most prospecting in California yielded nothing but dirt and hardship. A few on their way to seek their fortune decided the Arizona Territory looked promising, and these prospectors never made it to the end of the west; they started prospecting in the territory.

When lucky fortune hunters found a bit of color in Arizona, they mined it until it gave out. Glad to get what they did out of it, they moved on to their next "prospect." However, there were others, like Henry Wickenburg and the Schieffelin Brothers who hit it big. Although there were not many of those who found fabulous riches, their legends traveled far and fast, luring more who dreamed of the easy riches possible in the West. Gold and silver have always been mistresses with a mind of their own, and the byword of the early miners was, "Gold is where you find it."

The efforts of prospectors produced something besides mineshafts and dreams. If they found any promising ore, they set up camps. A strike drew other hopefuls as word spread. It didn't take long for a "tent city" to blossom. If the ore was good and plentiful, the mining camps turned into small settlements, and if a rich vein was uncovered, the men and women who made a living from the miners arrived. Businesses sprang up, many overnight. The fact that they were mostly saloons and brothels didn't make them less of a business. Gamblers, fancy ladies, and outlaws swarmed into the towns, and the exploding population brought the more traditional . . . cafes, grocery stores, lawyers, and doctors.

THE TIMELESS LURE OF GLITTER

Arizona's history is deeply rooted in her mineral and ore wealth. Historical tribes used her natural resources such as turquoise, silver, copper, and gold for trade and adornment. The Spanish mounted a number of expeditions in the 1600s and 1700s to search for the mythical gold cities of Cibola. While they found no golden cities, they did find a few ore-producing mines and a land of heathens in need of conversion to Christianity.

In the 1880s, Rafael Ochoa found plenty of evidence of early mining. He believed Indians and the Spanish worked the wash between Glesson and Courtland before the arrival of the pioneers. He found evidence of an old turquoise mine he was sure was Indian, as the Spanish cared little for turquoise.

In the Huachuca Mountains there is still evidence of lime slacking, an old Spanish mining method. The method requires a hole drilled one inch to one and a half inches in diameter and then filled with burned lime. After ramming in the lime, water is poured in the hole to slack the lime. Rocks plug up the hole, and the pent-up force of the slacking lime explodes, cracking the rock and loosening the ore.

Old-timers prospected by the formation and color of the hills and by signs of iron and other ore in rocks. There were plenty of these signs in the mountains of the Arizona Territory, thus producing a mining boom. Almost any showing of ore was an excuse for the sale of the claim as a mine. Promoters were numerous. They built mills whether the ore in sight justified such a move or not. After the mill was constructed, they would sell the mine at an enormous profit.

Prospectors followed the same course. Leaving the ore in their strikes when they saw it was not a paying proposition; they then were able to sell the mine to someone with more money than mining knowledge.

Prospector Rafael Ochoa spent most of his life looking for a big strike with little to show for it except enough to live on for a few years. Indians never troubled him during his prospecting days. They never stole from him, and often they would come into camp, squat round his fire, and grunt. Although they never asked for food, Ochoa was smart enough to feed them.

Once he hired an Indian to dig a trench. When he paid the fellow off, the Indian went to a saloon called Sodtown Crossing and got drunk. That evening, he came back asking for his pay. Ochoa gave him fifty cents to get rid of him, but he came back again. This time the miner ordered him to leave.

A little while later Ochoa heard a *thump, thump, thump* coming from outside. Investigating, he saw the Indian, so drunk he could hardly stagger, busily filling up the trench.

When prospecting in the Chihuahua Mountains, near Black Jack and his gang's hideout, Ochoa had a seventeen-year-old partner by the name of Billy Starbeck. The outlaws never bothered the prospectors; in fact they hardly spoke to them. Starbeck had a taste for bright neckties and fancy jewelry. One day, returning to their cabin, they found all of his doodads on the kitchen table. Horse tracks led to and away from the house.

It was easy to figure out that the Black Jack gang had planned to steal Starbeck's ornaments and then thought better of it. When Starbeck saw his things spread about, he completely lost his temper. He grabbed all the guns in the place and yelled he was going to clean up the whole gang. The prospector had a difficult time holding him back from sure disaster.

During his prospecting days, Ochoa knew by sight or acquaintance all the notables of Cochise County—the Earps, the Clantons, the McLowerys, Curly Bill, Black Jack, John Slaughter, and the rest. None of them paid much attention to him. He was only a prospector, often dirty, often unshaven, and uninteresting to all except a few of his own kind.

Charles Debrille Poston claimed to discover the first commercial mine in Arizona. He found silver in the Ajo District, thirty miles from

Tubac, and named his claim the Heintzelman Mine, after the major in charge of Fort Yuma.

In 1848, after the United States took possession of the land below the Gila River from the Mexicans, the first run of commercial ore taken from Arizona by Poston assayed for $760 a ton. His success came as a great surprise to his friends, who never expected him to survive his journey into the southwestern desert let alone make it pay.

By 1860 Poston's mines were yielding a thousand dollars per day, half of which was profit. His plant and equipment represented an investment of one million dollars. Few men could have engineered such a financial project in the pathless west.

In 1861 Poston's financial empire came tumbling down. The United States withdrew its troops from Arizona to fight in the Civil War. Chaos followed. The Indians went on a rampage, Mexican and American outlaws ran wild, and civilians were more interested in their own defense than that of a protecting a mining operation. Poston headed for the security of Tubac, closing down his mining operations. He stored around sixty thousand dollars worth of machinery at the Heintzelman Mine, paid the workers, and left for Arivaca with a Mexican guide, Mr. J. Ashburn, and Raphael Pumpelly of the Santa Rita Mines. They followed an old Indian trail to the Baboquivari plain. Their provisions consisted of parched corn, coffee, and sugar.

The tales of riches circulating all over the West and parts of the East drew Charles Gordes to Tucson in 1881. Although he had worked a number of different jobs, he never seemed to be able to resist the lure of prospecting.

"There is something about prospecting that is hard to break away from. Always the next hill will contain the ore, the next strike will be *the* strike, and the end of the next day will see the sun set on poverty." Gordes spent most of his eighty three years, either alone or with some partner, in lovely canyons, craws, and washes always looking for Eldorado while daylight lasted, and counting the stars at night before turning in for a few hours of dreams involving sudden strikes and rich ore.

Gordes's life was routine, as was that of most of the prospectors. They would plod out into the desert with a pack mule or two, some grub, perhaps a partner, and such tools they felt they would need. Months later they would return, and if lucky, they'd have a little money to spend. If not, well, it was back to getting a grubstake. They found amusement in the saloons, drinking and gambling, in which Gordes participated in a cold-blooded manner and with reason rather than indulgence.

Successful prospectors knew there were no mines in the roots of grass. You had to develop the mine and work hard. Even the hard work was no guarantee of success. Determination and tenaciousness helped.

Jack Durham recounted the story of a Dutchman in the Twin Butte country who owned a claim and was working on it for some time. Eventually disappointment set in and he abandoned the mine. Two fellows knocking around and not knowing a rock from a hen's egg, as Durham put it, were looking around the abandoned mine and stumbled on a seam. They were curious and sank the shaft deeper, just a little deeper. They found ore—gold . . . silver . . . copper. They sold the mine for twenty thousand dollars. With the introduction of mining machinery, the mine turned out to be highly profitable for the new owners.

LIFE IN THE MINING CAMPS

Joe Rothenhausler Junior, arrived in El Real de Santa when he was six years old. He spent the next thirteen years in one part or another of the Santa Rita Mountains prospecting with his father, Joe Senior.

Arriving in El Real de Santa Rita in the early 1880s, the Rothenhauslers found a thriving community. The district held four hundred or five hundred men. There were three stores, two small saloons, and one large saloon with all kinds of gambling games.

Americans owned most of the placer digging. The washing of the gold was mostly the occupation of Mexicans and Yaquis. Men arrived at the camp without passports or entry papers, crossing the international date line south of the old Mowry camp, now known as Patagonia.

There was plenty of money in the camp for gambling and buying drinks. However, when the placer miners sold their gold, they did not receive money; they received credit for store goods. The storeowners bought most of the gold and justified their credit-for-gold-practice by reminding the miners that they had to send the gold to the mint and then wait for payment. Payment in credit meant that the miner would only be able to "buy" what the storeowners had to sell. Since this was a universal practice in mining camps, the miner had little choice.

In gold mining camps, dry goods and groceries were cheap. Good meat sold for six or seven cents a pound. Beans were three to four cents a pound, Allison's Flour went for two cents a pound, and a new pair of overalls cost sixty cents to a dollar.

El Real de Santa had a curious custom. It was the habit to be kind and helpful to strangers and those on hard times. When Joe Senior, his wife, and five children arrived in the camp, they had food supplies for only a week to ten days. Very few jobs were available.

When the food was just about gone, Joe Senior said to a friend, "If I don't get work pretty soon we'll have to go back to Tucson. We are about out of food and my family has the bad habit of eating every day." The friend was appalled. "No, don't go back to Tucson. It is too hot down there this time of year. When our food is gone, we always start digging for gold. In El Real de Santa Rita the Earth feeds those who work." The father explained he had no claim in which to dig.

"When that happens here," replied the friend, "we go to someone who has a good pay dirt and ask him for a *garote* (a hit), because it is the spirit in El Real de Santa Rita, or because the owner fears that bad luck may come his way he may give you two bandanas of his dirt. So small an amount of dirt may give you forty or fifty cents, sometimes even more than a dollar when you learn how to scrape the bedrock right."

Joe Senior found some friends with good dirt and asked them for a *garote*. The friends never refused him the chance to try his luck. It was truly the spirit of the people in the district.

Ed Donner, one of the storekeepers, had some claims over in Boston Canyon. He offered to sell one of them to Joe Senior for twenty-five dollars. Rothenhausler told Donner that was over twenty-four dollars more than he had.

"Well," replied the storekeeper, "you can pay me from the gold you take out of the ground, and more than that, I'll furnish you with tools and a rocker, and food . . . and you can pay me for everything when you hit pay dirt."

The offer was accepted, and the next day father and son went to Boston Canyon to start a tunnel. It was for the most part unproven ground. However, before long someone down on his luck approached Rothenhausler for a *garote*. He even seemed pleased when some fellow stopped him and said, "Friend, I have no eats, how about a *garote*?" Joe Senior would quickly comply. If the man had a family, Joe Senior would often say, "Take two *garotes*, my friend. After all this is El Real de Santa Rita. There is always more gold in the ground." He felt as others did that granting this favor to another brought good luck.

Soon Rothenhausler was able to pay off the small claim (two hundred feet by two hundred feet), and then he purchased five others from Ed Donner. The gravel was not very rich, but it was rather wide and was from three to five inches deep on the bedrock. It was a matter of a lot of work for them to get enough gold.

These were days of hardships. Everyone ate what he or she could get of the plain foods the mountain stores had—meat, beans, and tortillas. Most slept on the ground. The houses were, at best, mere sheds roofed with dirt. Water was scarce and had to be carried long distances. Men and women worked hard and for very long hours, even small children did whatever work was possible for them to do. The only entertainment was the saloons and an occasional dance on a dirt floor.

When cold weather made living in the little jackal too uncomfortable, Mrs. Rothenhausler refused to stay. Believing he could continue to take out plenty of gold, Joe Senior took his wife and four children to Nogales, returning with his son Joe to El Real de Santa Rita. The two moved into a tunnel in Boston Canyon. It was much warmer than the little shack.

During the second summer in the district, they finished the last of the gravel pay dirt. They prospected on some of their claims and found some dirt that barely gave them food and clothing. Joe Senior was not satisfied with so little; he felt there must be more good pay dirt somewhere on his claims. He kept prospecting and trying to figure out how the buried channels ran.

When spring came, he found what he was looking for: A channel that was rich. Soon they were taking out gravel that gave from one to four or five dollars per box. Some of the test portions ran as high as twenty to twenty-five dollars per box. Forty cents to a dollar is good dirt, five- to twenty-dollar dirt is fabulously rich in any placer district.

Joe Senior sent to Nogales for his half-brother Juan. Juan was born and raised in Magdalene, Sonora, and was conscripted into the Mexican army and sent to eastern Sonora to fight the Indians. While engaged in that task, he met several of Sonora's bad men. One of his acquaintances turned out to be a good thing.

One afternoon Juan came running over the ridge. He had run more than two miles, but he was still scared. "Joe, Poncho Reveros held up and robbed the Lopez saloon and all the men. He saw me, and knew me. He nudged me and nodded me to get out just as he and his crew drew their six guns and called out, good and loud . . . Al cielo, Todas."

A half hour later, peeking out of their tunnel and through the brush, they spotted six mounted horses on the ridge, about five hundred yards away. The men looked over the country below them. Apparently satisfied with what they saw, they dismounted, built a fire, and made coffee. They kept two guards to the west and two to the east, and they ate in relays.

It was the Poncho Reveros gang, and his daughter was riding with him. He was dressed in the full regalia typical of an important Mexican horseman: a big hat, a loudly decorated buckskin jacket, big spurs, two guns, and big, full cartridge belts.

When the bandits finished eating, they went east along the ridge, down into the Louisiana Canyon, across Fish Canyon, and over the ridge toward Gardener Canyon.

About an hour later, the deputy sheriff and about fifty men, some on horses, some afoot, came to the top of the ridge where the bandit gang had made coffee. The posse tracked them on over to the Gardener Ridge, but never caught them.

Sheriffs never knew whom they would meet, and the sheriff that chased Reveros had another interesting experience with an outlaw about a year later. He was leaning against the end of the bar in the Lopez saloon studying a picture tacked on the wall several weeks before. In big letters at the top of the notice it read, "$5,000 reward for the capture, dead or alive . . ."

As the sheriff turned toward the gambling games, a smallish young fellow stuck out his hand and said, "Officer, I want to shake hands with you. Right there it says, $5,000, dead or alive. Do you want that money? I'm Billy the Kid."

The officer had already taken the hand, but he quickly let it go. "No-no-no! I don't want that money, no, no." With that declaration, he hurriedly left the saloon and headed home.

Before the end of the fourth year in El Real de Santa Rita, Joe Senior and his brother Juan had worked out the rich channel. When the rich pay dirt was gone, Juan went to Nogales and never returned.

Rothenhausler sunk hole after hole in Boston Canyon, but he never found one that paid. The prospectors were down to just beans. Finally one morning they ate their last beans. The men went out prospecting, but found nothing. One of the men killed a rabbit and borrowed some flour for tortillas, and that was supper. The next morning there was some weak coffee.

When the prospectors did not return at noon, Joe Junior put his saddle pack on his burro and headed for the store, hoping he could find something to eat for himself, his father, and the man helping his father.

He came to a small ravine where he often thought he might try panning the bedrock for gold. It rained the day before, and there was water in several of the little basins. He sent his burro, Leather-Hide, up toward the bend in the ravine and started prospecting. He found a place where the ditch made a sharp turn in the sand. There was a flat rock at the turn, tipped up a little, forming a pocket. Taking out a gold pan and short shovel, he lifted the rock away. He filled the pan with sand and went downstream to do the washing. When he had washed two thirds of the dirt over the side of the pan, he heard a familiar grating sound. Young Rothenhausler reached into the muddy water and grabbed a good-size heavy particle. It was a nugget.

When he finished panning the rest of the dirt, he had two small pieces of gold. It didn't take him long to arrive at Ed Donner's store. Donner weighed the gold out at $16.76. There wasn't a happier ten-year-old boy in the world.

He gave the storekeeper a list of items he wanted to take back to camp, and then he headed for a small nearby eating place where he demanded, "twelve bits worth of breakfast at once." At that the woman threw up her hands and said, "Breakfast, are you crazy? It's after three o'clock and you are asking for breakfast. Have you had no breakfast?"

"Yes, I had breakfast yesterday morning, but now I am hungry again. Do you hear me good mother? I'm hungry and I want twelve bits worth of breakfast. I want plenty of it, ham and eggs, coffee, tortillas, beans and whatever else you happen to have." The boy got his breakfast, and although it was a huge amount of food, he ate it all.

After breakfast he went back to the store and had the balance of his gold credit made into two orders, one to pay for the biggest breakfast he had ever eaten and another for supplies to take to his father.

As he approached the camp, his father noted the well-loaded burro and thought it was some prospector starting out with a pack of grub. Then he saw it was his son's burro, ridden by none other than little Joe. They used up that grubstake and some more, but they never did strike another pay channel in the Boston Canyon.

In primitive mining camps, danger came from aboveground as well as below for those who sought a life of mining. Living in the wild, it was a common occurrence for prospector Ignacio Calvillo to wake up with a rattlesnake in his bed or bedding. He was very lucky until the night he stepped out of his cabin and a rattler hit his foot. Limping into the light, he saw a pair of red spots on his big toe.

Growing near his cabin was a common weed called golondrina. Calvillo boiled the weed and applied it as a poultice, which drew out the poison. This medicine from nature saved his foot. Prospectors learned from the desert or perished, for they were always in jeopardy from weather, wildlife, outlaws, and Indians.

Not all early mining towns were wild. There was tranquility in Tucson's early days. Rafael Ochoa would frequently see women coming from the Elysian Grove carrying water home in ollas balanced on their heads. At night in the Old Pueblo, flickering fires in the hills surrounded the town as prospectors settled by their campfires adding a glow to the town.

The only work in Tucson then was with the mines. A miner worked nine to ten hours a day for a dollar a day. In 1901 a pay raise took the wages to $1.25, and $1.50, depending on the job.

At the San Xavier Mine, families lived in crowded living quarters consisting mostly of tents. They were placed up on the hill and were constantly washed away when a flood came careening down.

Silver Bell had a different look. When the Jerome Company brought in two thousand men, they cut up ocotillo, sahauro, and greasewood and built their huts. The government opened a school in the new camp, and a saloon opened up offering plenty of gambling and drink.

A traveling Mexican circus appeared. Huge bonfires lit up the performers as they swung on the trapeze and walked the high line. There were dances for the adults to the tunes played by harps and accordions.

The population of mining towns was a mixed lot. Most of the miners were Mexican. However, there were also Europeans, including a few Italians and a smattering of Slavs, Montenegrin, and Polish. The "Cousin Jacks" came from English mines and brought their wives, and some of the miners were Irish.

Robert Alexander described the pace of life:

After work, when the shift came out at three o'clock in the afternoon, the miners would flock to saloons and streets and start drinking. You would see Cousin Jacks with great jugs of ales; the Irish their whiskey and getting drunk; the Italians with their beloved wine, and the Spanish who quickly got drunk. For entertainment, we played cards, games for money like poker, Monte, and blackjack.

Stores were kept in all the mining camps where we could buy our groceries at very low prices. Coffee sold at three pounds for thirty-five cents, five pounds of lard also went for thirty-five cents.

When the rich ore played out, mining towns took another direction. Some, like Charleston, Ruby, and Helvetia, were deserted and became uninhabited lands of melted down adobe buildings left for nature. Tombstone, a wild town of sinful delights, gained its notoriety not for its ore, but for a gunfight that captured the public's imagination and piqued the interest of a society mad for old Western legends. Today, to the world, Tombstone is the town where the gunfight at the OK Corral took place.

A few defunct mining camps cashed in on the memory of their golden days. Bisbee and Jerome, former mining towns, managed to blend history with sustaining communities that draw tourists. Yuma became a city, but its main attraction is not as a historic mining town, but as the site of the territorial prison. Tubac is now a respected art colony and retirement community.

Not all the mining settlements failed or changed course. Morenci, Miami, Green Valley, and the Silver Bell area of Tucson are still supporting functioning mines.

Gold Is Where You Find It

John A. Hunt found his first gold in a pile of fertilizer. He was loading a wagon with the stuff on a stable floor, where the army kept Uncle Sam's mules overnight when en route from Holbrook to Fort Apache. The gold he found was minted five-dollar pieces lost by very careless soldiers.

Others, like Colonel Epes Randolph, a sensible man, knew that gold did not grow on trees, or usually in a pile of mule manure. Being an intelligent man, he applied science to the problem of getting rich. He hired a good mining engineer, a young man by the name of Prout from some university. Prout seemed to know about the earth and where good ore could be found.

At the time, Randolph was the superintendent of the Southern Pacific Railroad. At one time the railroad owned the old Yuma Mine. Randolph, now in possession of the rights, gave Prout a sample of the mine's diggings. The engineer examined the sample and pronounced it rich. He convinced Randolph to put forty thousand dollars into the mine. They sank a shaft to sixty feet and found nothing.

"Maybe I made a little mistake," Prout told Randolph. "Let us get a little deeper and I am sure we will strike it rich."

The colonel invested another ten thousand dollars, and they went lower, but still didn't find what they were looking for, so Randolph quit.

"Well let me tell you Colonel," said Prout, who was very sure of his geology books, "God Almighty did not do what he ought."

Prout's failures did not dim the ardor prospectors had for their hunt and dreams. Jack Durham summed it up when he said, "God Almighty

has not created any hombre that can see any further than the last shot
... the shot you blasted the rock with. What lies beyond no yellow-leg
engineer can tell. Geology is a good thing, but it has to be taken in doses."

The discovery of a vast deposit of gold, silver, and copper was a by-
product for George H. Stevens and his brother Charlie. They were among
a party of volunteers, led by Captain Chase from Silver City New Mexico,
chasing a band of renegade Apaches who had broken out of the reservation in the spring of 1871.

It was in the wilderness of what is now Clifton-Morenci-Metcalf
that they first uncovered the deposits. The Stevens returned in the fall of
1871 to work their mining interest. George soon tired of the mining business and turned his energy and attention to the cattle industry.

LUCKY TO BE ALIVE

At night strange noises came from the deep mine tunnels and holes. To
many the sounds were mysterious, but the miners knew they came from
the hundreds of field mice that called the tunnels home. These mice were
harbingers of trouble. When the mice ran out of the tunnels to the surface, no miner would go down, and those below would quickly come up.
The desertion of the mice meant gas. However, gas was only one of the
many dangers miners found below.

Cognizant of the dangers, Ed Welch's family persuaded him to get
out of mining. He did so with regret, as he would rather mine than do
anything else. His family had good reason to be worried. Fires, noxious
gas, falling objects, electric shocks, delayed blasts, and cave-ins are all
know hazards of a mining job. However, danger didn't always come from
what you anticipated. Sometimes a freak accident got you.

One day Welch was watching an ore bucket swing side to side as it
ascended the shaft. He looked down for a moment, and at that instant,
the bucket dislodged a wedge, which with accelerating velocity dropped
down, hitting him on the head and rendering him unconscious. It wasn't
his first mishap in the mine. Several times he was overcome by gas, and
once his air drill went into a hole previously drilled and filled with powder. Fortunately it missed the powder or it would have resulted in his
immediate death. Twice when trapped by cave-ins, he did not know if

rescue would come. On two occasions, he left his machine for a few minutes and returned to find a cave-in had completely smashed and buried his machine under several tons of rocks, right where he had been working.

When Ed Welch worked the small mines in the Chihuahua Mountains at elevations of 7,500-plus feet, electricity would run down the air cables and water pipes during thunderstorms. Often the miners would be working with air drills while standing in water. Several times, knocked way from his drill, Welch suffered painful wrists and swollen feet from the shock. His clothes would be soaked with sweat after his working shift. In the winter it was common for his overalls to freeze solid by the time he reached his home, a mile away.

A miner had to be on guard for signs of trouble, even subtle ones. While working at the Hilltop Mine, Welch noticed that the carbide lamps were burning unusually low. The flame was only an inch or two from the opening. The miners lit a candle. It promptly went out, indicting noxious gas in the area. From then on the miners kept candles lit in the tunnels to help them detect gas. "When the candles went out, we went out," reported Welch.

There were no large mines in the Chihuahua Mountains in eastern Cochise County. A lot of the prospecting was with one or two men working. These mines usually paid for a while, then the ore would run out or become so low in percentage it became unprofitable to work them. Lead and zinc commonly bound together in these mines and were often hard to separate in the smelting process. When one predominated, the smelter charged the miner extra for the difficulties of separating the metals.

Welch and a partner leased a property that had been previously worked. It contained copper, lead, and silver. Initially they made a living, but a cave-in brought this enterprise to an end. Both men were in the mine at the time, replacing the old timbers when boulders, weighing several tons each, came down all around them. Again Welch escaped injury, but his partner wasn't as lucky. His injuries kept him from working for several months. The cave-in proved too expensive to clear, so the partners abandoned the mine.

Welch lost a friend when he fell from a ladder and broke his back. Another time a delayed blast imbedded a large rock in the chest of a miner working near him. That same blast blew another man to bits. Welch helped pick up the pieces, "a piece of jumper here, and a wad of hair on the other side of the tunnel . . ."

Fire was a danger miners had to work with. In the Bisbee Mine it was a constant threat. The high percentage of sulfur, often at 85 percent, is what kept the fires burning. Compressed air, pumped into the tunnels, kept the burning coals from dropping on the workers, like fire through a stove grate. One day, though, the blower went out. The twelve miners working in the area avoided the raining fire by seeking shelter in a nearby air chamber.

The ore fires in the Bisbee Mine were constantly burning, but not nearly as fierce as the Jerome fires. John Hand described the conditions in Jerome: "These fires would smelt the ore and in Jerome they took steam shovels and scooped out the ore after the fire had been through it."

In the Jerome Mines the intense fire created a deadly gas that was a constant hazard. You could smell gas from the fourteen hundred and fifteen hundred levels on the ten hundred levels. The steel rails, used in firefighting, would turn red hot.

The primary method of fighting the mine fires was to smother them. The mining company did this by throwing up bulkheads made by placing mesh wire against the side of the tunnel and spraying fine cement on to it. This produced a thin concrete veil that protected the miners in passing and confined the fire to definite limits. However, noxious gas would often find cracks through which to escape.

Fire wasn't the miners' only worry. Mine owners had to contend with water levels, too. When they struck water in Tombstone, it came in with such a rush it drowned out the mine and seriously slowed working the rich ore. Pumping equipment was a solution, but the cost of pumping equipment, including labor and fuel, was enormous.

Due to the fissures in the underground rock, if one company pumped, it lowered the water level in all the mines. Other mines profited by escaping the pumping costs. This slowed the mining operations, as each owner waited for another owner to start pumping.

This waiting game created an intolerable increase in the water level of all the mines. Finally the conditions became so serious that the mine owners joined and installed a Cornish-type pump that threw out millions of gallons of water each day. It was at one time the biggest pump in the world.

The stressful and dangerous working conditions produced a miners' humor all its own that played out in unusual ways, and at odd times. The Hilltop Mine, discovered and sold by John Hand, was the site of one of these unique incidents. The Hilltop had one tunnel that went through the mountain. It was about a mile long. Doors on each end of the tunnel were to contain the wind, which blew through with a gale velocity so strong it would extinguish the lights.

One day one of the workers came through this tunnel with his arms full of cigars and bottles of whiskey. He was half-drunk, having sampled the whiskey during and after purchasing it. Helped along by the wind, he bumped frequently into the walls. Bruised, he arrived at his destination with broken bottles and cigars so soaked in whiskey they could hardly be lit. That didn't stop the miners from enjoying their drinks and smokes.

There is nothing glamorous about a miner's job, and in the 1800s safety rules, if they did exist, were haphazardly enforced. It was hard and dangerous work, and the pay, although steady, was low. For Ed Wittig the pay depended on the values recovered from the ore that day and usually ranged between three and four dollars a day.

Wittig, a mucker in the Tough-nut Hole mine, worked underground for more than a year in an atmosphere smelling of pungent gases, with tunnels that could be dry or damp on any given day. He lived with the uncertainty of never knowing if he would rise to the surface from the four-hundred- to five-hundred-foot levels. His workday was never less than ten hours, often much more.

The skill, knowledge, and dependability of the miners varied. Not all the miners were cautious or knew what they were doing. Robert Alexander found some to be reckless not only with their lives, but with the lives of others. One day two crews were blasting in crosscuts. Alexander told the other crew not to touch their dynamite until his crew had passed. Just as they went by, the other crew set their dynamite off, blasting Alexander. He sustained severe head and face injuries, which earned him a hospital stay of over eighteen months.

Alexander knew from childhood the dangers miners faced. His father, an Indiana coal miner, died in a mining accident. Yet mining gets into your blood, and he started his mining career when he was a child and worked at the trade his whole life.

The mining profession offers no security. You are at the whim of nature and big business. Whether the mine is a small one, owned by one or two prospectors, or a huge operation owned by a corporation, it is difficult to predict when a vein will run out and a mine will close down. Faced with nature's arbitrations, Alexander, like most miners, moved from mine to mine working in Kingman, Miami, Ajo, Bisbee, Morenci, Twin Buttes, and Dos Cabessas over a forty-year period, until the Depression put him out of work. Another, Rafael Ochoa, also moved from mine to mine. He worked the Old San Xavier, Hughes Mine, Silver Bell, Tumacacori, and Salero Mines. E. D. Welch found employment in several mines, including the Hilltop Mine, Paradise Mine, and George Walker's Leadville Mine in the Chihuahua Mountains.

It Takes a Special Man

The sparsely populated West, where the law was mostly the gun, called to certain types of men. Men who were independent, mostly loners, and lived life the way they chose without bowing to conventional behaviors or society's rules.

Lars Haagensen was such a man. A big Norwegian, he arrived in Prescott and worked the area before deciding to try his luck in Bisbee. He traded his burros and other gear and bought a bicycle. He rode and walked the six hundred miles into Bisbee in fourteen days. He was quite the sight freewheeling down the Mule Mountain Pass. He claimed the distinction of being the first bicycle owner in Bisbee. Haagensen started in the mines as a mucker and worked the mines for forty years.

One night when he went into the newspaper office to pay for his subscription, Haagensen discovered he had lost his tobacco pouch. He decided to run a classified advertisement to see if he could recover the pouch.

Haagensen looked to be in poor financial condition, and the thoughtful newspaperman suggested that before he spend the money on the ad, he might want to retrace his steps. Remembering he was at the post office just prior to visiting the newspaper office, Haagensen rushed off to check that area.

He returned with a greasy old tobacco sack bulging with paper bills. He unwrapped a ten-dollar bill, which seemed to be the smallest denomination in the roll.

"How much money do you have in the pouch?" he was asked.

"Say tank ay got more den sefen hunert dollsre."

"Great Scott man, you shouldn't carry that much money around with you, someone might rob you."

The wise Norwegian asked, "You tank you be robber?"

"No, of course not," replied the affronted newspaper man.

"Vell, you and me is de only ones know diss."

Haagensen decided to leave his money to the president of the Miners and Merchants Bank, who was also president of the Shasttuck-Denn Mining Company of Bisbee.

His newspaper friend was astounded. "My gracious sakes man, that fellow has millions now. He doesn't need any more."

"Yust the same, he do me a good turn couple times when ay was sick. Ay nefer forget mine old friends. He gave me a yob and ven ay vas sick, he paid de bill, and by golly von time he buy me a pair of pants von my ass was sticking outside."

Haagensen lived to be eighty years old, despite the fact that he smoked the strongest tobacco in a dirty old pipe and ate garlic by the pound. When they laid him to rest, an entourage of cosmopolitan society followed his cortege to the Bisbee Evergreen Cemetery.

For over forty years, Max Shultz led a solitary and isolated life on Humbug Creek in Yavapai County. Because he saw so few people, he retained his heavy foreign accent. He worked Humbug Creek and nearby Minnehaha Creek as a placer miner. When the placer goal ran out, he turned to prospecting for hard-rock veins.

His cabin, located about ten miles southwest of Crown King, was noted for rich pockets of gold and silver ore, and Shultz had his fair share in finding these pockets.

Once he struck a rich pocket of ore that amounted to four burro loads and assayed out at ten thousand dollars in gold and silver. The mineral was rich in silver. Small pieces of the pure mineral were 68 percent silver with 15 percent antimony. The antimony heated out with a blowpipe broke down to a button of pure malleable silver. This was not the first pocket Shultz found, but it was the richest and put him on easy street for the rest of his life.

In a dry wash, just north of his cabin, erosion has uncovered a big vein in an outcrop of rusty-looking quartz that stood at least fifty feet high above the wash. The low-grade vein was between thirty and forty feet wide. When mining developers look at property, they judge the mine by the richness of the ore and the accessibility of the site. Shultz's property was difficult to get to, and the ore was of a low grade, yet, like most prospectors, he kept up the work hoping to make the sale.

When he became too old to mine, Shultz spent his time walking over the hills, looking for ore pockets that were easy to work. He did location work to hold the claims and then tried to sell them. Every Sunday, Shultz put on his Sunday best clothes, got a clean shave, and waited, just in case he had visitors.

Dick Gird and his partners were among the very few who struck it rich. Soon after the Schieffelin Brothers and Gird found Tombstone and exposed its vast wealth, buyers from the East approached them and offered them large sums of money for their holdings. The Schieffelins, who probably had never earned more than $3.50 a day in their lives, were afraid to take on the future, and against Gird's wishes they sold out their part for about a hundred thousand dollars. This crippled Gird, but he was just Irish enough to be visionary. Although always a poor man, he hung on, made millions out of the mine and mill, and then sold out for an immense fortune. To everyone's surprise, he figured out what the Schieffelins had lost by selling early and wrote them a check for that amount. To him a partner meant something.

Gird installed a distilling plant at his mill, which provided plenty of free ice and distilled water for all. However, the men working for him figured that the process of distilling removed all the natural salts in the water. Knowing salt was necessary for good health, they distained the free water for drinking purposes, but did use the ice to cool down their "healthy" drinks.

When Gird made his big strike, he had to keep going with old equipment so he could repay the sums he had borrowed to start his mine and build the smelter. Reworked five times, the mine turned out to be so rich that the tailings and slag from the first mill produced a profit as big as the original ore.

Gird built an immense office building of adobe; the walls were almost three feet thick. In this, he installed a large steel safe to protect the precious bars while they awaited shipment to the US Treasury. He papered the walls inside the building to hide the ugliness of the adobe mud. A wise man, Gird never put a bar of the precious metal in the safe. It was a bluff. He dug out hiding places for the smelted bars at various places in the walls and hid the holes with removable panels covered with wallpaper.

The task of freighting the ore from Tombstone to Charleston was a problem for small outfits. Finally a man named Durkee took over the contract for a large fee and made it work. At the end of the first year, his books showed an immense profit, so he decided to throw a party.

He hired the biggest saloon in Charleston, bought all the liquor in the place, and then had more sent in by railroad. The girl entertainers got a fixed price for the night. Piled on the gaming tables were huge stacks of freshly minted dollars. A large orchestra came in to entertain. Everything was free.

Only workingmen were invited. The admission was a blue flannel shirt. Both miners and freighters wore them as part of their working garb. All the white-collar employees, bookkeepers, officials, and tin horns were barred from even approaching the place.

When the crowd had finished off the imported wines, brandy, and rum, they started on the "common soldier's whiskey." This stuff was sure to knock a man sideways at sixty yards without a miss.

The men outnumbered the hostesses; the latter complained they were being danced to death. The amateur croupiers and game tenders lost immense sums to the players. Joy reigned supreme until sometime after midnight. It was then that the freighters, who were mostly Texans, felt they had to tell the others about the woes of their native state during Reconstruction. The miners, who were mostly Irish and Cousin Jacks, advised them to forget it and enjoy the night. Forget Texas?! No more dastardly insult existed.

Luckily, the men were searched for guns when they entered, but table legs, cuspidors, and bottles made punishing weapons. Finally the Texans were heaved outside and the party was over. The next day, Durkee paid for the plate glass mirrors and the other broken fixtures. Although he made lots of money in future years, he never threw another party.

Dogged determination is almost a requirement for prospectors. William Kirkland seemed to have more than his share. In 1865 he was a farmer with a good crop of beans, corn, and potatoes when the Indians came in and stole all of it. To add more insult, they also stole all of his livestock save for one burro.

Farming was impossible with one burro, so Kirkland decided to go prospecting. His poking around led to the discovery of one of the richest mines in the Old West. It was of free gold quartz. Kirkland set up an arrastra and worked the burro to grind the ore. His labor of two months produced two thousand dollars. One day, before he left the mine to travel the four miles home, he hid his gold. As he approached his house, he saw Indians surrounding it. His wife was fighting to protect the house and family. He opened fire on the Indians. Now facing attacks from two sides, the Indians retreated. Placing his children on his burro, and with Kirkland and his wife walking, they headed for Skull Valley, where they knew there was a camp of US soldiers.

The next morning the soldiers and the Kirklands started for his property only to find, when they got there, that the renegades had stolen everything in the house and then set the fire to the building.

Kirkland was afraid to return to his mine without protection. He finally persuaded the soldiers to go with him so he could pick up his gold. The only thing left of the mine was the adobe walls.

Kirkland and his family settled in Prescott and it was over a year before he could get back to his homesite and rebuild. He returned to his mine, and the Indians jumped him again. The fight that ensued lasted several days. Finally, soldiers arrived and chased the raiders off.

Determined, Kirkland moved his family back to Skull Valley. Leaving them at the fort, he went into Prescott to get supplies. He was broke after his years of hard luck and he needed credit.

There was only one store in Prescott. He had dealt with them for years. He went in and asked for credit, and the storekeepers said no. He left the store and went out to his burro and his shotgun. Driving his burro into the store, he made his point to the owners with his shotgun.

"Boys load this burro up." The owners quickly complied agreeing, "All right, Mr. Kirkland, come back when you need more supplies, we know you will pay us just as soon as you can get your mine working."

Kirkland agreed, "You are right boys. I will pay you if the Indians don't get me. But don't never let me hear of you fellows refusing credit to a rancher or prospector again."

Kirkland went back to mining with three partners, Moose Langley, Tapman, and Alfred Shupp. Kirkland, Shupp, and Langley did the mining work while Tapman kept a lookout for Indians from atop a granite peak. Today the peak bears the name Tapman Lookout or Tapman Peak. They successfully mined enough ore to locate several ranches in the area. Kirkland paid off his debt at the store, but both storeowners died poor with plenty of unpaid account on their books.

Alexander McKay came to the Santa Catalina Mountains of Arizona in 1878 to join his friends Albert Weldon and Jimmie Lee at their Oracle Mining Camp, named by Weldon after the ship in which he sailed around the Horn.

McKay arrived at the camp riding one mule and packing another. Since there were no houses in the area, McKay slept under a fly tent. One morning while he was baking bread in a Dutch oven in front of his tent, he heard a whistle. It was a weird sound considering he was miles away from everyone. Looking up, he spotted an Indian making his way toward him who kept shouting at him, "Me George. Me Eskiminzin's man. More come. Eskiminzin come." Topping the ridge was a band of Indians made up of women, men, and children.

They had two quarters of venison tied on their pack. They told McKay they wanted some flour, and McKay was wise enough to know they would take the flour anyway, so he offered to trade for a quarter of venison, and they agreed. He became disconcerted when they camped right beside him, and the next morning, instead of prospecting, he sat on the hill where he could watch his camp all day. They did not disturb anything and soon moved on.

Prospecting knows no holidays, and it was on Christmas Day McKay located the Christmas Mine. The next week, he found another mine and appropriately called it the New Year. By that time, he was sick of living in the open, exposed to Indians, snakes, and wildlife. He decided to build himself a house. There was nothing in the area at the time but game trails and Indians. Building the first house in an area that became the town of Oracle earned him the title of "The Father of Oracle."

McKay had a pet bull snake that would follow him to water. One day a visitor came in, excitedly exclaiming, "My God, boys, I just killed the biggest snake I ever saw right at the door." So much for pets.

In 1878, Weldon, Roark, and McKay located the Wadsworth Mine. In 1883 McKay found the Peer and the Peerless, the mines that started the Quihotoa District booming.

When they first explored the area, McKay was not feeling well and debated climbing a high steep mountain that looked very promising. It was a difficult climb, and Weldon finally stopped and declared, "By George, Mac, I wouldn't go any further if the top of the mountain were covered over with twenty dollar gold pieces." So he started down. It could have been pride, or determination, but McKay refused to stop and continued climbing.

The first rock he knocked off was a quartz blowout. That became the Crocker. Then he knocked off a piece from a ledge, which looked to be rich in horn silver. When they took it into town to have it assayed, Weldon said it would never go over fifteen hundred ounces. It went forty-five hundred.

Coming back from the assay office, McKay ran into W. C. Davis, who had a little tin shop on the southeast corner of Main and Congress in Tucson. Over the years he had been good to McKay. Once, when McKay had received five thousand dollars for the sale of a mine, the storekeeper kept the money in his safe and let McKay draw it out when he needed it. When showed the assay results, Davis asked to come in on the mine. Weldon agreed, but at first Roark, the other partner, said no. Finally, Roark was convinced, and Davis was located in. Eventually Don Cocker, Maxwell Bruce, Herbert Tenney, and Richfield came in on the extension with McKay. They shipped thirty-five thousands dollars worth of ore from the mine to Argo, Colorado, before they sold it to James Flood and the Comstock Nevada outfit.

McKay was in San Francisco when he met Flood, who wanted to know what he could get the Crocker for. McKay said there were five partners, and they would want ten thousand dollars apiece. Flood said that was too much, but McKay knew he would pay it. When he got home, McKay told the partners to sit tight; they did, and received fifty thousand dollars for the mine. The Comstock people put a mill on the property and ran it for two years. Then the vein began to widen and the values dropped, as it was impossible to sort the good ore from the poor, and the company abandoned the whole project.

In boom times, McKay's Quijotoa mining area was a camp of about three thousand people with churches, gambling houses, and even a newspaper called the *Silver Bullion*.

Shortly after the McKay's house was finished, the Watermans settled in the area and started a cattle ranch. Then, the Dodges, who were running a rooming house on Main Street in Tucson, arrived. They constructed a one-room adobe and called it the Arcadia Ranch.

The area was growing. Isaac Loraine and Bill Henecke settled at the American Flag and struck some good ore—silver and lead. There was a big white ledge near the American Flag, but no one looked at it until Mrs. Loraine, who was on her way to deliver her husband's lunch, stopped to rest on the ledge. Idly she broke off a piece of the ledge and found free, course, heavy gold. She located a claim and sold it to a company that put up the first mill.

It wasn't long before a stage was running from Tucson to the American Flag. About this time, the Dodges turned their sheep ranch into a boarding house for people suffering from consumption.

THE PROSPECTING GOVERNOR

In 1871, exciting stories of rich deposits of gold and silver, told by a man named Miner, had just about every pioneer man thinking of prospecting. They convinced Governor Anson P. K. Safford to join an expedition of over 250 men to mount a prospecting venture in the Arizona Territory. Five companies formed, and the governor was the leading spirit of this venture.

Safford's company of thirty men started out from Tucson under the guidance of Miner, who asserted he could guide them to a place where, from a single shovel of earth, he had panned out more than a pound of gold. Edward G. Peck headed up the Prescott delegation. Other famous men lured into the wild for this epic hunt including William Rich, Al Sieber, and R. W. Groom.

Starting out from Camp Grant, the prospectors, drawn from Phoenix, Florence, Tucson, and the Sonora, marched to the San Pedro, then on to the mouth of the San Carlos. They followed the river to its source, crossing at the Salt River, where they spent some time prospecting. Next the expedition moved to the Tonto Basin and from there to Cherry Creek, where they settled in, spending a considerable amount. They prospected in the Sierra Ancha Mountains, but found neither silver nor gold. Returning to Cherry Creek, their next route was down the Salt River, where they crossed to Wheatfield's, and explored Pinto Creek.

By now the prospectors realized that Miner's story was false. Dishearten, the men separated and returned to their communities, poorer than when they set out. It was the largest, and most thorough, expedition that ever went prospecting in Arizona. The wonder is, with the land they covered, they never made a strike.

The quest for gold was not the only get-rich scheme Safford faced. In 1871 a Kentuckian named Arnold and his partner, Slack, salted a mine with twenty thousand dollars of African and Brazilian rough-cut diamonds. Slack did some prospecting right after this and "found" a few gems. They displayed rubies and diamonds in New York and San Francisco, claiming the diamond mine was located in the neighborhood of Fort Delance, Arizona. In reality, the salted mine was in Colorado at the extreme northwest corner of Arizona. This was an excellent choice by the men perpetuating the fraud, as the area was rich in garnets, crystallized quartz, and brilliant petrifactions.

A company, with ten million dollars in capital, secured three thousand acres of land, and there were plans to work the claims and to sell shares to the eager public. Visits to the location produced some fines.

The swindle caught not only the public, but also many prominent businessmen, in its net. A few Arizona citizens were involved in this diamond fraud. In July 1871 a suspicious and cautious A. F. Banta went out to make a study of the fields. Banta studied the situation for about six weeks. Upon returning to Tucson, he reported to Governor Safford that the diamond find was a fake. The US Government also sent distinguished geologist Clarence King out to evaluate the situation. He too proclaimed it a fraud.

LUCKY CUSS

Ed Schieffelin had about as humble a start as any man. He was born in the coal-mining region of Pennsylvania and brought up in the gold-mining region of Oregon. As a child looking for gold, he used a milk pan to wash the sand from the creek next to his log cabin home. When he was twelve, he ran way and joined the gold rush to the Salmon River. By seventeen he was a seasoned prospector and decided to try his luck in the West.

As a civilian scout in 1877, Schieffelin rode into a land described as "a wilderness land of ambushed death." Geronimo and his warriors were on a rampage out of their Dragoon stronghold. As a member of Al Sieber's flying squadron of scouts, he and the other scouts made their headquarters at Camp Huachuca. It was from there that Schieffelin mounted his mule and set out on his prospecting explorations.

He stopped in a little valley a mile east of the San Pedro River at the old Brucknow house. Frederick Brucknow was a German scholar and scientist exiled from Germany for his involvement in political activity in the revolution of 1848. He built the house, a long three-room adobe, in 1858.

Brucknow began digging a mine near his home. When it reached grave depth, an Indian arrow toppled him into it, dead. A succession of prospectors took up the mine digging, looking for the reported vast treasure located there. Seventeen men lost their lives there; none found riches. Some say the spirits of these old prospectors still wander around the house and mine.

Sitting on a pile of rock at a campsite in the mountains, Schieffelin told Sieber he was going to dig in the old Brucknow mine. Sieber scoffed at the idea, telling him he would not find ore, but only his "tombstone" in the mountains. Schieffelin was determined and set out with his mule to prospect. Undaunted by incredible hardships, hostile Indians, and the discovery of skeletons of unlucky adventurers, he continued his search for evidence of ore.

He followed a dry wash to the hills, and when it split, he stopped pondering which fork he should take. A cottontail rabbit darted from a covert and scurried up the right-hand gulch. On a whim, Schieffelin staked his mule and followed the rabbit. It was there he found the silver ore, some of which would assay out at two thousand dollars a ton. When he made his big discovery, he had just twenty-five cents in his pocket. He spent that on tobacco and started his slow journey to Tucson to file his claim and find his brother, who was working at the McCracken Mine. Dick Gird was the mining engineer and assayer at the McCracken. When he assayed the ore, he made an offer to finance the venture for a partnership.

The Schieffelin Brothers set up camp at the Brucknow place. Al Schieffelin was the cook, Gird the assayer, and Ed the prospector. Gird built a crude assay furnace.

One day the prospector returned from a prospecting trip, jubilant and shouting, "I've struck it rich this time." His brother replied, "You're a lucky cuss." They named the mine the Lucky Cuss.

Another claim was located, and they called that one the Contention because of the dispute with other prospectors over ownership, which they settled by compromise. Schieffelin then found the Tough Nut, which was rich in horn silver. Almost overnight the town of Tombstone evolved and became one of the greatest silver-mining camps of the West.

They sold the Contention for ten thousand dollars, and the buyers took millions from it. They sold half their interest in the Lucky Cuss, and the other half made them rich. The Schieffelins sold their two thirds in the Tough Nut for a million dollars. Gird later sold his third for much more.

Ed Schieffelin went to New York to live, then moved on to Washington and Chicago. He traveled extensively and met many distinguished people. His adventuresome spirit took him to the Yukon on a steamer he built for himself, but his hunt for gold there was unsuccessful.

He returned to California and married Mary E. Brown. He built her a mansion in Alameda overlooking San Francisco Bay, and still he was restless. Next, he bought a residence in Los Angeles and seemed content to settle there.

However, Ed Schieffelin was a prospector and a wilderness man at heart. He returned to the wild, to his cabin in the Oregon forest, and that

Prospector Ed Schieffelin
KEITH DAVIS COLLECTION

is where they found him dead on May 12, 1887. He was lying face down and stretched out full length on the floor, dressed in the rough clothes of a prospector. A tramp hound lay whimpering at his feet, a pot of beans had boiled down to a charred mass, and the bread in the oven was burnt to ashes. As he wished, he was buried in prospector's garb, with a pick and shovel, and a canteen beside him in the coffin. A tower of rough stones marks his grave.

MADNESS, MILLIONS, AND MYSTERY

Henry Wickenburg was the kind of man you never forgot. Considered a character by many, mad by a few, and certainly a mystery by all, he lived by his own rules. One old-timer remembers the day he met Wickenburg, a day he will never forget. He was driving his buggy up to Wickenburg's store. His wife had sent him out for ten pounds of sugar. It was a typical Arizona summer day, hot and hellacious as only desert temperatures can be.

As he approached the store, a big, fairly well-dressed man leaped from the store doorway, moved across the porch, and half-turned on one of the three wooden steps to the road. A shot cracked out from the store and the man spun around two or three times, came down a step, and fell flat on the road. Confused, wanting to avoid trouble, the observer didn't know what to do. The man just lay in the street, bleeding a bit.

The buggy driver hitched his horse to a post away from the store, just in case there was going to be more trouble coming out of that doorway, and walked over to the man. There was no doubt he was dead. One shot through the chest on one side, with the bullet obviously entering his heart. The driver didn't spend any more time observing the body; he headed into the store. It wasn't any of his business.

The store was quite dark after the brilliant sunshine, and it took a few moments for his eyes to adjust. A long counter stretched from one end wall to the other. Behind the counter were shelves stacked with goods, and above the counter hung all sorts of objects. The counter had obviously spent its previous life as a bar, and it gave the store a saloon atmosphere. Behind it sat a small man figuring out accounts. In front of him, off to the right, lay a revolver, its barrel pointing to the door. The man lifted his head and blue piercing eyes looked out from under thick eyebrows. The buggy driver was face-to-face with Henry Wickenburg.

From this event, one would think Wickenburg was a cold-blooded killer. Rather, he was a man who had his own way of doing things, and his name was good enough that nobody ever questioned him as to why he shot down a man on the steps of his own store.

He was a contradiction of characteristics; he may have been tough and ruthless, but he also had a kind heart and showed this gentle side as often as his rough one, as one rancher learned. The man was living in Phoenix and found he could not support his wife and five children there. He faced financial ruin and decided to move to the far side of the town of Wickenburg to start over again. The family set out with their wagons, horses, cattle, and other livestock. It was a difficult trip for the family, as his youngest was still nursing and his wife was ill.

Wickenburg was the only man he knew in town, and that was a slight acquaintance. He asked Wickenburg where he might get some food for his animals and shelter for his family, while he went on to find a place he could fix up for them. Wickenburg ordered the family to move in with him—his wife, children, cattle, and livestock. The livestock went into his pasture, the wife and children into his home.

It took the rancher a lot longer than planned to get his new ranch in shape. Wickenburg fed and sheltered his livestock and family for nearly half a year. When the rancher came to move his family and possessions to his new little ranch, he felt embarrassed; there didn't seem to be any way to set a price on all Wickenburg had done for him. Of course he expected to pay.

The rancher's oldest daughter asked on the day they were to leave how much Wickenburg wanted for all he had given. The family offered to leave behind the fattest of their cows and a couple of horses he had admired. They would leave these as partial payment.

Wickenburg glared at her, "Do you want me to slop your face?" When he was angry, his German accent took over. The daughter was shocked at his anger, and admitting it wasn't much, promised her father would pay more once the first crops sold. The wife, wiser with years, understood. Tearfully she explained to her daughter, "Mister Wickenburg means we are not to pay anything."

In 1847 Henry Wickenburg worked his way to America from Prussia as a fireman on the steamer *Cortez*. In 1852 he went to California and found work in the placer mines at Ophir, not far from Auburn. He earned enough to start his own business. Not afraid of hard work and challenges, he dug the first artesian well in California.

In the early 1850s news spread of the gold discoveries in the placer fields around La Paz, on the Arizona side of the Colorado River. Wickenburg tried but had no luck there. He heard of a party of explorers who had headed for Tucson a few days earlier. He decided to join them and overtook them at Peeples Valley, traveling nearly two hundred miles alone through Apache country. When he left Peeples Valley, he continued with the party east to Walnut Grove, then on to Turkey Creek and Black Canyon.

He heard from King S. Woolsey about the rich ore in the Harquahala Mountains. With Van Biber and Greene he started out for the mountains. They followed the Hassayamp River, then set out across the desert for the place Woolsey had described. They were not sure of finding any water until they reached the pass in the Harquahala Mountains where the gold was supposed to be. This meant a stretch of fifty miles and back with only the water they carried. In October 1863 they discovered the cropping of the Vulture Mine. Van Biber and Greene had little faith in the find and took off for Tucson, ostensibly for more supplies. They never returned.

Gold is where you find it, and Henry Wickenburg found it where it should not be, according to the knowledge of the time. Prospectors found gold in creeks, where it washed down and concentrated in the riffles of the stream, or in ledges of decomposed granite, but it was never sticking up above the surrounding country. Experts said you had to dig for gold. Scores of prospectors and experts had looked at these mountains, but never thought there was any gold around.

Wickenburg climbed up the mountain, away from prospectors who were searching in the creeks and valley, and saw this mineralized vein protruding. He chipped off a piece, and there in his palm was a nugget weighing about eight ounces.

However, Ignacio Calvillo offers another version of the discovery of the Vulture Mine. He says Wickenburg's Mexican sheepherder found the gold. The Mexican was wandering on top of a hill and found a piece of rock full of gold. He didn't know what it was, but he knew it was unusual. He showed it to Wickenburg. When Wickenburg realized what the rock was, he gave the boy a gun, some money, and a horse and sent him off.

Wickenburg staked out all that the Arizona law allowed, a three-hundred-foot claim, then two others, each three hundred feet on either side of the discovery claim. He piled up his discovery monument and corner posts. He knew he'd struck it rich, but he didn't know he was walking on about sixteen million dollars worth of gold—all within easy reach.

Wickenburg began working the mine in May. He built an arrastra in July 1864 and managed to get a ton of ore to his campsite. When C. B. Genung visited Wickenburg's camp, he was shocked at the primitive arrastra Wickenburg was trying to use. He showed Wickenburg what he could about the method, remolded the existing arrastra, and helped him grind a ton of ore. From that ton, they took seventeen and a half ounces of gold.

In less than twelve months there were forty arrastras running on Vulture ore, some with burros and some with horses, mules, or oxen. Wickenburg furnished the ore, for which he charged fifteen dollars a ton. Between 1865 and 1866 there were four mills within one mile of the town of Wickenburg.

Henry Wickenburg sold his discovery claim to Bethnel Phillips in 1865 for eighty-five thousand dollars. He sold the two other claims for fifteen thousand dollars. A hundred thousand dollars was all he got for his find.

Wickenburg settled in the town with his name and spent his years running his store, and doing some hunting when he got bored. Even in his later years, Wickenburg was a tough man. Bored with his storekeeping, he decided to go hunting one day. He didn't care what he shot: bear, mountain lion, deer . . . it didn't matter to him. He took his old smooth bore breechloader, which he refilled with his own shells. The combination didn't always work well.

The first day he killed a buck and hung it from an oak bough. Wickenburg had trouble sleeping that night, and when he glanced out of his tent, something yellow caught his eye. He heard the crunch of teeth on the buck's carcass.

He headed for the wagon to get his gun. He knew the yellow he spotted meant the critter was a mountain lion. He wasn't frightened, he was mad. Just as he got one foot on the wagon wheel, he felt something sniffing at his right leg. Slowly he looked around into the eyes of a bear. As he pondered his next move, the bear sniffed up the leg and down, then swung around, and went over to the dying fire. By now the lion had dragged away the carcass and Wickenburg had his gun, but he couldn't find a shell.

Then right at the edge of the clearing, he spotted a mountain lioness and four little cubs. He sat in the wagon cursing. If it hadn't been the first night out, he would know where his ammunition was, but right now his stores were in a muddle. His mutterings and moving around woke one of his companions. That startled the animals and they left.

By sunup Wickenburg, his dogs, and a companion were after the bear, mountain lion, and lioness. The trail led to a narrow wash set between wooded hills and rocky buffs that overlooked an almost dry creek. Wickenburg had no idea if he was following the lions' or the bear's trail. It didn't matter which animal, he had his smooth bore with him loaded with a round shot. At close quarters it was just as effective as any weapon against a soft-bodied animal.

Hoping he was following a lion's trail, Wickenburg carefully checked the rocks and long grass growing in the dry creek bed, places lions like to rest in the sun. As he stepped into the creek bed, he spotted lion tracks heading for the grass. He didn't want to send the dogs, he was afraid they would get in the way of his shot, or the lion would kill them.

There was a breeze blowing up the wash, and Wickenburg decided to fire the grass. He sought high ground while his companion started the fire at the lower end. There was a rock wall behind him, with not much of a foothold, and at sixty-five, he was not as limber as he once was.

The grass caught fire, but the roots were green and smoke spread out like a fan. Walking away from the center of the smoke was the lioness and her cubs. Wickenburg got ready to fire, but the rolling curtain of smoke hid the animals. Hot sand and smoke, filled with red sparks, dimmed his vision.

The smoke poured up and seeped into the crevices and holes between the big boulders, and that's where it found the bear, which was nestled in the rocks, above him. The smoke cleared a bit and Wickenburg moved to a spot where it seemed the thinnest, and here he spotted the lion, the father of the family, between him and the rocks. Now Wickenburg has a bear above him in the rocks, a lion between him and the rocks, and a lioness and her cubs in front of him. He took his best shot at the lion, knocking him over with a bullet that broke his spine. The beast lay there, glaring at him. He went to reload only to discover that his shell case had burst and left a bit of its material sticking in the breech.

Henry Wickenburg stood there, in a hunting stance, with his legs wide apart, trying to ram in the shell, and then trying to pull it out. Suddenly, through the smoke, the lioness and her cubs appeared in front of him. She headed for her dying mate, then spotted Wickenburg; she lashed her tail, narrowed her eyes, and glared at him. Wickenburg started to slowly step back while continuing to bang at the shell until his hand dripped blood.

He tripped over something soft; it was one of the cubs. The lioness sprang for an attack while Wickenburg reeled to one side, cursing and hammering away at his jammed shell. If necessary, he was ready to run the gun barrel down the animal's throat. Much to his relief, the lioness picked up her cub and carried it to the rocks where the others were scampering to safety.

It was Wickenburg's chance to escape. However, he felt he was getting the worst of the deal and he didn't like that at all. He got out his extractor, pulled out the jammed shell, reloaded, then roughly bound his bleeding hand with a piece torn from his shirt sleeve. Now he was ready to follow the lioness's tracks into the rocks. He thought he had lost her when he came to a narrow stretch lined with boulders that ended in a big green bush. He threw a rock at the bush—and a bear came out.

Smoke was blowing all over the area, which annoyed the bear, who now intended to take out his mood on Wickenburg. The hunter set himself, aimed, and fired. The bear quivered, then came hurling at Wickenburg, who stepped between two boulders. The bear shot over the ledge and landed heavily in the creek below.

Wickenburg loaded another shell, a prickly between his shoulders made him look up. Glaring down on him was the lioness. She'd hidden her cubs in the rocks and was climbing over the boulders where Wickenburg was wedged. He flung the barrel up as the lioness reached over to fish him out, and pulled the trigger.

The ball went through her throat and lifted out the back of her head. The recoiling gun almost tore off his fingers. The lioness slumped down over the edge of the rock, and the two were jammed together between the rocks with Wickenburg underneath wondering if she were dead. However, she bled a good deal down his neck before the blood coagulated, and he was convinced she was dead. When his companion arrived, he had squeezed out of the rocks and was peeling off his coat. Cheerfully Wickenburg told him, "Bring the dogs, and the cubs I will also shoot."

In his last years he got involved with spiritualists. They told him they could bring people back from the Great Beyond, and could create eclectic ectoplasm. They made other supernatural claims that he believed too.

One night Wickenburg walked away from his house and into his fields, and he met his death. The coroner's jury brought in a verdict of "death from gunshot wounds," a verdict that explains nothing. Some whispered that he had killed himself; others wanted to lynch the spiritualists. The man who had braved ferocious wild animals, the man who found millions of dollars, died mysteriously as a pauper. He feared little, except perhaps himself.

THE LOST MINE OF DEATH

The storm sent a chill through the pretty part-African, part-American woman as she rushed through the streets of Phoenix. As she passed Dick

Holmes, she called out, "Mister Ho'mes, will you go ovah to our house? Ole Dutchman, he 'bout to die." Holmes rushed to the old Dutchman's house and sat next to the bed of the dying man. That is where he heard the story, told in the dying man's last words, of the rich mine of Jacob Wols. A mine that would become the legend of "the lost Dutchman's mine."

Wols (or Wals), with his dying breath, told how one day in 1870 he set out from his camp, near where Roosevelt Dam is now, to meet some men from the village of Florence. He realized that if he cut across the Superstition Mountains, he could save himself many miles of travel.

Six miles from the river, an Indian's arrow, shot from an ambush, nicked him on his arm. Familiar with the ways of Indians, he ducked and ran. He hadn't gone far when six Apaches jumped him. A fierce fighter, he was able to fend them off, killing three. When nightfall came he escaped by crawling some distance. Once he felt he had lost them, he walked several miles to widen the distance between himself and the Indians. When daylight broke, he realized he had no idea of where he was. Not only was he lost, he had no water—a deadly situation in the desert.

Logic told him that if he followed the dry washes and canyons, they would lead him back to the river. Realizing he was in a life-threatening situation, suffering from thirst and hunger and exhausted by his encounter with the Indians, he struck out down the washes. By noon he was barely able to continue, and that's when he spotted a faint human trail. It led to a point near a huge, dominant, pointed oval rock. Heading for the rock, he rounded a knoll and saw three Mexicans. He staggered into their camp gasping, "Water! Water!"

Although surprised, the men immediately went to their kegs; he drank greedily, and then ate an enormous quantity of food, which they offered him. Only after that was he able to rest and take in his surroundings. He wanted to know what they were doing in the wilderness.

"Par el oro, senor. The gold we get here, the mine, it est ours." Wols told them there was no gold in those mountains. The Mexicans, insisting there was "Mucho oro," proved it by taking him to their mine.

They enthusiastically bragged about the richness of the mine, and took old Wols to the nearby diggings, showing him the outcropping of ore and the rich veins in the quarts they were collecting.

Wols was astounded. For ten years he had prospected in Arizona, and the best he could do was to do a little sly high grading from other miners. Yet here before his very eyes was the richest, most unbelievable bonanza he had ever seen. It was beyond his most exaggerated dreams.

By pretending complete ignorance of mining and ore, he was able to inspect the property carefully. He fingered bits of rock, his eyes gleaming with avarice. He asked the Mexicans numerous questions, gathering as much information about the property and mine as he could. In simple faith and hospitality, they answered him.

They had no way of knowing that this stranger with the flowing white beard, the one they had extended the most generous of hospitality to, was a deadly shot with pistol and rifle. They also built their confidence on the fact that they outnumbered him three to one.

Jacob Wols brought his rifle with him on the mine tour. In his belt he had tucked his pistol and knife. The Mexicans' guns were propped against their little lean-to shack by the side of the red rock cliff. The old man edged away from the Mexicans until there were several feet between them. Suddenly he cried out with alarm, "Ain't that some men a-coming yonder?"

The three miners turned to look, and Wols calmly picked up his rifle, stepped to one side—putting two of the Mexicans directly in line with him—lifted the gun, and fired. The two men crumpled, the scream of one ripping the air with its horrible sound. The third quickly turned toward Wols, yelling "NO, NO, in the name of . . ." He never finished the sentence; the second shot quieted him forever.

When he was convinced they were dead, he dragged their bodies about 140 yards to a deep and narrow crevice, dumped them in, and piled rocks on top of them. Finishing the burial, he went back to the mine, collected a double handful of the nuggets, and squatted, staring at them for a long time. Jacob Wols's greed and cruelty started a trail of killings that lasted into the 1930s.

Wols collected all the gold he could that day and headed for Phoenix. There he celebrated his riches, and as any prospector would, he got rip-roaring drunk. The drunker he got, the more belligerent and louder he became. "I got a private graveyard in the mountain, and I'll fill it up yit.

Got enough gold to pave this street, and I'll blow hell out any man that tries to steal it." He bellowed and bragged. When a drunk mentions gold, others listen, and when he backs it up with a bag of proof, they begin scheming. Loafers plied him with questions, but learned little. A drunk with a good poke is asking for trouble, and when he left Phoenix with three burros and a complete set of tools, even a fool knew where he was going.

Wols was a canny and sly man. The fourth night out he built a campfire, ate supper, then took his blankets over to some scrubby bushes and settled in for the night. Two hours later, from down the draw, half a mile behind him, quick shots cut through the silence of the night. The blankets were a decoy. Two weeks later cowboys found the remains of two well-known Phoenix men. Wols didn't always kill his pursuers. Sometimes he just wore them down. He would set up camp, spend his days panning some gold or backtracking, throwing his shadows off the trail.

Then came the day when two soldiers made the same mistake the Mexicans made. At first they outwitted Wols and tracked him right to the location of his mine. Feeling safe, because they were two army men to one civilian, they shouted at him as they ran down the steep mountain slope toward the mine. It took Wols only a few seconds to rid the world of these intruders.

The body of one rolled down over the rocky incline, stopping at the murderer's feet. The white-bearded devil calmly tied a rope around the legs of his victims, hitched them to a burro, and dragged them to the same crevasse he had dropped the Mexicans.

Other men who were able to find the Dutchman's mine came to mysterious deaths. One, after finding the mine, returned to his camp for tools, went into his mineshaft to collect his favorite pick, and died when the shaft caved in. A man named Deering also found the Dutchman's mine and returned to town to drink and brag about his new potential riches. He became so obnoxious that a fellow drunk drove a dagger through his heart. End of riches, end of Deering.

Wols finally decided he needed help in working the mine and fending off the many intruders. He felt he could only trust his family, so he sent for his nephew Julius.

Julius was overwhelmed with the riches of the mine. All he could do was talk about how he would spend the money. When they reached Phoenix, he became a spendthrift, and within a month the two had to head back to the mountain for more gold. Julius continued boasting and bragging, until one night, making camp, Wols had had enough. He picked up his rifle and put a bullet through his own nephew's head. He tied a length of chain around Julius's neck, dragged the body a few yards, and buried it in the sand under an overhanging lip of rock.

Jacob Wols died in Phoenix, killed not by a claim jumper's gun, but from pneumonia. Even the clever, cruel, and quick could not outsmart Mother Nature.

Before Wols died, he gave Holmes several clues to the location of the mine.

The key is a stripped Palo Verde tree with a pointing arm, one big limb left on. It points away from Weaver's Needle. About half way between it and Weaver's Needle, and 200 yards to the East, is the richest gold mine I ever heard of. When I was up there the last time I covered up the mineshaft. I put heavy ironwood logs across the opening, piled rocks and dirt on top of that, then planted a cactus on the spot. The gold is still there, not far from Weaver's Needle.

Strangely, the deaths in the hunt for the Dutchman's mine did not end with the death of Jacob Wols. Several people have gone to the Superstitions Mountains looking for the mine and have never returned. Skeletons turn up now and then, including the beheaded body of easterner Adolf Ruth in 1931. Finally, for the sake of safety, and to preserve the land, the government forbids all prospecting in the Superstitions Mountains.

CHAPTER 3

Cowboys and Shepherds

We fought thieving Indians, white rustlers, and other brands of out-laws, drought, disease, and low markets, and everything else that can happen in cattle country. Still we managed to keep our feet on our own ground and come out on top in our old age.

—WILLIAM THOMAS SANDERS

The iconic figure of the Old West is the cowboy, depicted usually as adventuresome, courageous, and brave. We read about him in our novels, we worship him on the big screen, and we make heroes out of many of the historical figures, romanticizing them.

However, the reality of the old Western cowboy is much harsher. For the small independent cowboy, with his own ranch, it was hard work and often deep disappointment as he faced complete or near financial ruin and many life-threatening situations. It took great determination—and the ability to defend his property from outlaws, Indians, and wild beasts—to succeed. When starting out, many of the young men never knew about these hardships, or they chose to ignore them, and consequently suffered greatly for their ignorance. Some never recovered financially or physically.

A merchant can lock up his business and leave it. A miner can shut down his diggings and walk away. The rancher doesn't have those options. He cannot walk away from hundreds of head of cattle, and he can't shut them down. Ranching is constant work. It knows no season, and part of the job is roundups, branding, cattle drives, and selling the cattle, all labor-intensive job requirements and all at the whim of Mother Nature.

Ranching isn't just about the cattle. There are ranch maintenance chores—the fences to replace, the repair and maintenance of equipment, the water resources—that all leave a rancher with little time for anything other than his ranch responsibilities. Cowboys don't work on the clock, but from the start to the end of a task, with roundups and cattle drives the most important events. Because of the long hours, and the many requirements and skills needed, ranching is usually a family affair.

However, for all of its challenges and uncertainties, life on the ranch is not bad. Tom Wills felt he had sufficient food on the hoof, tame or wild, but he did miss his green eatables. He stocked his dugout storehouse with canned goods, ham legs, bacon, flour, potatoes, beans, and other things that would store well. When they butchered a steer, they stocked up on jerky, which they boiled, broiled, fried, or even ate raw. The mountains supplied them with deer, antelope, turkey, and quail, and sometimes bear. There were even times when they had milk from their range cows.

According to Bert Lee, before 1864 there wasn't a cow in the country. There were just patches of ground where men grew market garden stuff. They would do their farming in the daytime, getting back to town when the sun was low. When the early independent ranchers arrived, they had only their ambition to start with. First they had to find a potentially promising location and apply for homesteading rights, which allowed them a section of 640 acres.

Their shelters originally were simple sod homes. The more sophisticated dwelling, such as adobe or rambling wooden ranch houses, came after they settled in. Early ranchers, such as Bert Lee's father, made their own joists, beams, and window frames. Builders made shingles by choosing a pine tree and chopping out the heart. Lee split the quarters into two-inch-thick pieces. Heavy stones on top of the roof kept the shakes from blowing away. Lee, like most pioneering ranchers, used wooden pegs that he made as iron nails cost too much and were hard to find.

In the southern part of the territory, most ranchers preferred the simple Mexican-style dwellings of adobe. They formed the bricks of mud and dried them. The adobe houses were one or two rooms, considered big enough in the old days for any size family.

Finding stock for these ranches was easy. There were herds of cattle roaming on the open range in Mexico. These wild cattle were supposed to have originated from a small herd that managed to escape from an Irish freighter wrecked on the Gulf of Mexico in the fifteenth century, although many said they were the offshoots of animals brought by the Conquistadors.

A few of these herds drifted into the mountain regions of the Arizona and New Mexico Territories. These cattle were small-boned black or spotted animals with sharp horns. This livestock, ranging in the desert and mountains, was anybody's property. That is, anybody who could corral and brand them, which was not an easy task.

A good roper with an iron could get himself a start in life by branding a bunch. However, he had to be very good with both rope and pistol, as these brutes were fighting wild and often gored both the horse and the rider. A pistol came in handy whenever a lone rider needed to save himself because a bull, rider, and rope became hopelessly tangled in the mesquite and the bull was hooking everything in sight.

Of course out on the range occasionally a tame, gentler calf got in the way of branding, even if the roper knew it belonged to some other settler. This invariably caused trouble, and some wranglers resorted to guns to settle matters. In the old days there was no cattle sanitary board to handle such problems. Cattlemen solved them on the spot by whatever means available.

INDEPENDENT RANCHERS

When Texans overgrazed their land and began looking for greener pastures, they headed north into the Arizona and New Mexico Territories. Here these former Texas ranchers found plenty of good, free grazing land, wide-open spaces, and little law to harass them. Young men, hoping to make their mark as cattle barons, joined experienced ranchmen, and Arizona became dotted with independent ranchers. For them, unlike the syndicated larger ranches, it was hard years until they could show a profit. Many did not make it. The more persistent rancher, who found creative ways to stock and finance his ranch, was the successful one.

In 1876 Samuel Green, at the age of ten, was a top hand on his father's ranch near Safford. Their range stock was Kerry cows, better known as Mexican wild cattle. The family made a living out of these cattle for years. However, when Green was in his early twenties, the price of cattle was down to six and eight dollars per head, and he decided it was time he went out on his own. No range cattle for him; he had saved some money and decided to buy a good herd. He chose a homestead site out in the desert called Polecat Springs, about twenty miles from Duncan. Initially he didn't need to bother with fencing. It was in a remote area where there was plenty of free range, and fences were not required in the early years.

Green bought 150 feeders from various cattlemen. He went up the Blue River and bought two fine Hereford bulls from rancher Toles Cosper. He paid three hundred dollars for them and considered himself set up in the cattle business.

Some of the early ranchers got off to a slow start. Although Edward Vail started his ranch in 1882, he wasn't prepared to take care of a herd. It wasn't until 1884 that he began stocking the ranch. He bought his first six hundred head from a New Mexico drover named Miller. They camped near Benson, the pickup point. That night the Indians stole their horses. One man aroused the camp and followed the Indians, but they had disappeared into the Whetstone Mountains. Fortunately for Vail they did not bother the cattle.

In 1884, Vail struck a deal for several cows with John Slaughter, who ranched near San Bernardino. The next year he added to his stock with the purchase of a few Mexican cows at thirty dollars a head. Vail had to be content with whatever he could find, which was mostly Mexican cows, as there wasn't much else around. Eastern cattle were hard to find, until the Percy Brothers, who managed the J. H. Ranch, had a few shorthorns they were willing to sell.

Albert West, who started out as a puncher with the Tin Cattle Company, decided he would rather work for himself than someone else. With his brother Bill, he started a livestock feeding business in Yavapai County. For a seasonal per head fee, they fattened up cows, grazing them in their lush pastures. Eventually they got tired of only feeding cattle. They quit the business, selling out their herd of 680 horses. The brothers moved to Tonto Creek and established the Griffin Ranch.

Tonto Creek wasn't the safest place to settle at the time. It was the stomping ground for criminals for miles around. Al and his brother knew that the best way to keep out of trouble was to mind their own business. They asked no personal questions, they solicited no information. Keeping the code of the West, they were hospitable to every rider, inviting visitors to "rest their saddle."

The outlaws showed their gratitude by cleaning out the brands on both sides of the West ranch, but leaving the brothers alone. They knew the Wests saw nothing and heard nothing. That didn't mean there were no confrontations with visitors. One day two strangers rode up. The Wests were breaking horses, and one of the strangers commented on the nice stock. The stranger pointed out two of the horses and said, "We'll take those two horses, cut them out and put our saddles and bridles on them." Al took exception to this high-handed manner. "Well, I don't know about that, I haven't said I wanted to sell those two." The stranger clarified, "Never mind what you haven't said, just cut them out and put our rigs on them."

It was about one hundred yards to the house, and none of the men working had guns. Before the strangers rode away on their new horses, Al asked them for pay. One of the men laughed and asked how much the horses were worth. Al thought about fifty dollars each. The stranger said, "Well now, I may send you the money sometime." With that vague comment, they left.

Six months later a cowboy rode up and asked if two strangers had bought a couple of horses from them a while aback. Al told him he guessed so, he sold a lot of horses. "Well," said the cowboy, "two men told me they got two horses from you and gave me this hundred bucks to pay for them." Some transactions took a lot longer in the Old West.

Jack Durham was another young man who saw his future in cattle. He started ranching in Pinal County in 1899 with sixty head of cattle. Like many new ranchers, Durham supported himself by working at something else. For him, it was his mining claim. His wife Lily would go down the shaft and fill a bucket, and Jack would pull it up. It was hard going and produced a very meager income.

Things were grim just before July 4, when the Durhams headed for Mammoth to get supplies. They were hoping they would come across some game they could shoot so they could use the meat to barter for supplies. The wagon and the .30-30 rifle were about all they had. There was no money. However, Lily did have a silk quilt she planned to raffle, hoping this would bring them much-needed cash.

Luck was with them that day. Durham shot two antelope, and Lily made $147 on the raffle tickets. While in Mammoth, they sold a third interest in their mine for two hundred dollars cash and fifty dollars in groceries. Lily's quilt was such a success that she wrote back East to friends and relatives and asked them to send their worn-out silk dresses. From these she made more quilts, sold or raffled them off, and in two years was able to add eighteen hundred dollars to their earnings.

While the Mexican cattle were free, for a ranch to have some hope of success it needed a better grade of cattle. Durham built up his stock by purchasing a few head from Marshall Hickey. Hickey was a mining man, and a deputy sheriff. One of his jobs was collecting taxes. Many a frontiersmen had little cash and paid debts with whatever collateral there was. For cattlemen it was usually some of their stock. Durham was able to get a fine calf for fifteen dollars and a red heifer for twenty. Nine months later the heifer gave birth to a bull calf, which he sold to a Florence butcher for sixteen dollars.

The Durhams were not the only early ranchers who had to find ways to support themselves until they turned a profit. When his ranch business was slow, Joe Winsor went to work for Ben Pascoe, driving oxen and logging for Pascoe's sawmill operation near Globe. When that didn't pay enough, he hired himself out as a hand to Andy Blankenship, the foreman of the Flying H. He was paid thirty dollars a month and supplied his own saddle.

When Claude Nichols and George and Charlie Smith (whose right names were Hill) decided to grow a little spread of their own up on Blue River, they figured the easiest way to stock their new ranch was with mavericks, since it wasn't a crime to brand them. If they weren't sure whom every maverick they found in the woods belonged to, they couldn't see where it was necessary to try to find out. They figured they were doing the community a favor by slapping a brand on them. Unfortunately, that cavalier attitude got them in trouble with the law, who went after them. They headed for the timber and got lost in the woods, but not before Charlie caught a bullet in his shoulder.

Tom Wills agreed with Nichols, "Stealing is when you brand a calf that still is following its mother. It's easy to tell a weaned calf. If you cannot tell if a calf has a mother or not, the calf according to the custom of the range belongs to the one who owns the range."

However, Wills preferred a safer, less dangerous way to stock his ranch. To start his herd, he traded his wrangler wages for stock. When the outfit he worked for went broke, he had enough cattle to set up his own.

When the drought struck Arizona in 1890, hard-hit cattlemen began selling out. Wills bought Emerson Stratton's Pandora Ranch. The ranch house, a wooden cabin built by Stratton on the side of the mountain, was in good condition. Near it was a dugout, which was Stratton's first home on the ranch. It made an ideal storehouse for Wills.

Wills built a drift fence, although it was against the law to fence in government land, and consequently he got into some trouble over it. The Interior Department told him to tear it down. Wills explained how it would mean maintaining line riders night and day. Realizing Wills's predicament, the Interior Department decided they were not in a hurry, and if Wills would consider their letter a second notice, they would not push the issue. The fence stayed up until Wills sold the property.

Wills came up with a plan that enabled him to make use of the free wild cattle and earn money for better stock. He had a contract supplying beef to mining camps for nine cents on the hoof. His outfit killed the wild cattle, packed them on mules, and turned them over to the camps. The profit went toward buying better stock and improving his herd.

Mark Hicks was one of the more successful independent ranchers. He learned how to manage his stock from his Texan father, who came to the Arizona Territory in 1887. The senior Hicks increased his herd by "mothering." He had a few extra good milk cows, and as there was more milk on the ranch than needed, he decided to make the cows raise more than one calf per year. Hicks bought baby calves from the dairy and then trained the cows to mother them. The dairymen did not want to be bothered with the calves and were more than willing to let them go for a low price.

Never a Safe Moment

If the hard work didn't get you, Mother Nature conspired with other factors to get you down. Ranch land was in remote areas, where bobcats and lions and wolves and coyotes were a constant problem. They would hunt down calves or isolated cows. When the ranchers found a victim, they buried it immediately where it was unless, for some reason, they had to get the carcass out of there. Then they hauled it away to an appropriate spot. Cattlemen considered this just one of the hazards of ranching life. But when a wild animal showed up practically on their doorstep, that was a different situation and the hunt was on.

When Jack Durham was out watering his cattle near his ranch house one September morning, and his dogs set up a ruckus, he knew it was a danger signal. He had seen a cat in the area now and then, and figured the dogs must have gotten the cat's scent. He didn't have his rifle with him, but he picked up his .22 hoping to scare off the animal. He saw the dogs had cornered the bobcat on a cliff. The cat was pacing back and forth, occasionally prowling to the edge to snarl at the dogs.

Durham discovered this was a special cat. It was the biggest cat he had seen in these parts. He didn't hold much hope that his puny .22 would be much help, but he thought if he could bust the cat's eyes, he would at least hurt the beast. This was a dangerous maneuver, since a wounded cat could leap at the dogs and start fighting. Durham took his shot, and the bullet entered the corner of the cat's right eye and went through the skull. When Durham went to haul the body away, he found how special this cat was; it weighted in over one hundred pounds.

Indians were one of the biggest problems that plagued ranchers. They struck without warning, burning down homesteads, killing settlers, and stealing cattle and horses. The ranchers who had spreads near the reservations knew they were in peril if their stock roamed on Indian land, but having your homestead far away from the reservations was no guarantee of safety. Bert Lee's father was keenly aware of these Indian dangers. He frequently spent his nights alone and knew he could not fight off the Indians. To protect himself when alone, he added something special to his house. He dug a hole beside the hearth and laid a long stone over it.

During Lee's second year at the ranch the Indian' attacked. He drove them off with the help of some men riding nearby who had heard the shooting. After that, the Indians started stealing his horses. He decided to lay a trap.

Lee tethered a horse down near the lake. He took a needle gun, which fired a .50-caliber bullet two or three inches long, and he waited for the Indians.

Two Apaches crawled up to the tethered horse. Lee let one get into view. The Indian made a perfect target, highlighted by moonlight. Lee fired. He missed. He started to reload, and the gun jammed. The Indians left, firing a hail of arrows as they departed. In disgust, Lee threw down his new needle rifle, whipped out his old six shooter and blazed away. It was too late for accurate shooting, but he did find bloody patches in two different places, indicting he had wounded both of them.

The next year, the Apaches attacked in force. Lee got under his stone. The band drew close, racing around the house and yelling. They shot burning arrows at the house, which stuck under the shakes and set the house on fire, but they did not try to break into the house. They waited outside, hoping to shoot Lee down as he raced from the fire, but his hidey-hole, with its stone cover, protected him from the heat. They left thinking he was dead.

Their belief that they had eliminated the rancher emboldened the Indians, and a few days later they rode to the ranch house in daylight. Again, Lee saw them coming and took refuge under his stone. He fixed the cover by supporting a section of it with a log so he could see out, and he lay there with his gun watching them as they approached. When he thought they were close enough, he starting shooting and was able to kill the chief and two others. The Indians hurriedly left, confused and bewildered, not knowing where the shots were coming from.

Samuel Green, who was born in Safford on June 6, 1866, grew up on a ranch and learned to be always on guard. His caution—and a special horse—saved his life. For his twentieth birthday, Green received a horse that was foaled on the reservation. For some reason the horse had a hatred of Indians, he couldn't even stand the smell of them.

On December 1, Green headed for Clifton and was about twelve miles out of Solomonville. Riding up a dry wash, suddenly his horse Bingo almost jumped from under him and bolted into a run. Green knew what had spooked the horse. There were Indians in the area.

By the time he got the pony under control, he spotted a band cutting across the mesa about a mile from him; they were going hell-bent for leather. He was too far away to see if they wore war paint. Hiding as best as he could behind a big clump of cactus, he watched them ride off into the same wash he had just left behind.

Although the Green ranch had very little trouble with Geronimo and his tribe, the sight of those Indians scared the young man half to death. He was afraid to ride away, and afraid to hang around. He peeked into the wash and saw more Indians had joined the first bunch, and that they were now driving a herd of horses.

When he could no longer see the band, he worked around and got on the trail toward Clifton again. He didn't want to turn back for fear he might run into the Indians. After traveling about six miles, he met Seth and Alonzo Wright riding in a high lope. He could see they were mad as hornets. As soon as they saw the cowboy, they drew rein and called out, "Ain't seen any Indians have you Sam?"

Green told them about his near encounter, and the Wright Brothers told him it was their horses the Indians had stolen. They also gave him news of Geronimo going on the warpath. They were determined to get their horses back if it was the last act of their lives, and they asked Green to go with them.

Like a lot of frontiersmen who survived by following their hunches, Green had a feeling that told him to decline the invitation. He tried to get the brothers to turn, but they were too fired up and insistent on going after the Indians and their horses.

The nervous and wary young cowboy continued on to Clifton. By the time he got there, the town was buzzing with the excitement of the Indian uprising and the news that Geronimo was on the warpath. The Indians had already killed several people, hitting ranches hard from the Black River to

Lordsburg, New Mexico. Among the dead was Mrs. Pipin of the Triangle T Ranch located twenty miles above Clifton, and a man by the name of Widdon from the Triple X Ranch above the Blue River.

Several days later Sam Green learned of the murder of Seth and Alonzo Wright, killed only a few miles from where he had met them. If he had gone along with them, he would have died.

Incidents that fueled the fire were occurring all over the territory. When the Indians killed a cowboy in Cibecue, Globe Sheriff De Voris went with some deputies to arrest them. When the lawmen arrived, the chief reached out, took De Voris's reins, and made a grab for his gun. The lawmen opened fired and killed the chief. This skirmish exacerbated the problem, as the rampaging Indians took to the trail, traveling back and forth from San Carlos to Cibecue, inciting the other Indians to war.

Rustlers or Indians did not bother every cow outfit, or settler. M. P. Snow worked for the Chihuahua Cattle Company for thirty years as a puncher and never lost any cattle to rustlers, and he lost only a few to Indians who wanted the beef to eat. However, he did find the Indians to be a nuisance, if not dangerous. "The Indians were friendly, almost too friendly. They begged for everything they saw . . . things to eat, things to wear, old saddles, bridles, everything," he complained.

On long drives, or hauling freight, Snow's outfit always tried to make camp near an Indian village, hoping that would make the Indians perceive them as friends. They knew that if they camped at a distance from an Indian camp, the Indians would try to steal the outfit's horses at night.

Not all Indians were on the warpath. Many were friendly to the settlers, and some even worked for the cattlemen. The problem was that sometimes the pioneers couldn't tell the dangerous Indians from the safe ones.

Lily Durham was at home fitting a dress for a friend, when her ten-year-old adopted son threw open the door and fainted in fright. Coming to, he pointed weakly toward the window, "Indians," he gasped. His mother ran to the open window and saw two Apaches approaching. She snatched a gun and aimed at the nearest one. Her friend Lizzie shrieked and threw up the muzzle of the gun. "No, they're Pete Young's Indians."

Aware of the danger, the Indians threw up their hands shouting, "We good Indians. We Pete Young's Indians. No shoot, we good Indians." El Coyote and Little Jack were there to sharpen their knives on the brimstone by the window.

Little Jack's squaw was a big woman who wanted to do nothing but boss around Little Jack and watch him work. He did all the work in their shack. He even washed all the clothes using amole roots for soap. He cooked the meals; she ate the biggest part.

The Indians had a sense of humor, which usually was unappreciated by the white settlers. On one of his trips, Joe Winsor was the victim. He was on his way from his ranch to his herd, and crossing the Salt River about sundown, he fell in with a band of traveling Indians. When they stopped for the night, he decided to camp with them.

He tied the rope on his horse to his saddle and lay with his head on the saddle, close to the fire, and went to sleep. Sometime during the night, a hot coal brushed against his heel. With closed eyes he reacted by kicking out, sending the coal toward the fire.

In a few moments, he felt another hot coal on his heel. Again, he kicked it back to the fire. When it happened a third time, he opened his eyes and discovered one of the squaws was scraping the coal against his heel for a joke. When the moon came up, he saddled his horse and headed for his herd.

Stockmen could earn a good profit with hard work, but hard work could not compensate for the lack of rain and the death of the grass. The drought that struck the San Pedro country was quite severe. For two seasons there was not a drop of rain. All that was left of the gamma grass, that once covered the mesas, was seared roots. By 1890 the plains and hillsides were nude, burned up by the sun.

These were hard years for the cattlemen, and one after another they went broke. A whole herd would lie down and never get up again. There was no feed for sale. Some ranchers took what cattle they could up to the mountains where there was an inferior graze, but it was all they had. Unfortunately a large number of this stock went wild. That happened to Emerson Stratton. He took twenty-five hundred head up to the mountain and lost most of them when they became wild.

Easy Money

There was easy money out there on the range for the dishonest man, one who didn't much care if he made his point with his fists, or with his gun. These men had no liking for the routine of regular hard work, but instead wanted the quick dollar. The quickest dollar for ruthless and amoral men was rustling.

Cattlemen were aware of the danger of rustlers, especially when they were on the trail. For their part, the rustlers knew they would meet stubborn resistance, and they prepared for it. Their biggest advantage was surprise, and their larger numbers. They had the twofold goal of killing the guards, or night riders, and keeping the restless cattle from straying away from the bed grounds while they stampeded them.

When cattle are alarmed in unfamiliar country, especially at night, they very quickly become panicky. The cattle hightail it away from the racket that has disturbed them. Often it doesn't take a large stampeding herd in rough country more than two minutes to get out of sight. Herds would have a long start before sleeping drovers could get up from their rough beds, saddle up, and go after them. Meanwhile the cattle were scattered in all directions.

Before attacking the herd, a few members of the rustling gang took positions that would enable them to guide the cattle in the direction they wanted them to take. After the stampeding herd had run for a while, and the outlaws had it under their control, a number of rustlers would stop at a good ambush spot and wait for the trail drivers who were chasing after the stampeded herd. These unlucky cowboys met a hail of bullets, wounding some and killing others. Sometimes the regular trail drivers never gave up until there was no longer any hope of recovering their cattle. Unfortunately, there were many cases when the whole herd was lost—rustled and sold by the outlaws, earning them plenty of money for very little effort.

Not all the cattle thefts took place on the trail. Sometimes ranch locations bred some unique cattle-stealing schemes. The California and Mexico Land and Cattle Company had four thousand acres of fine land in Sonora, Mexico, just a few miles from Cochise County, Arizona. With the adjoining national land, they could run over thirty thousand head of cattle.

Dick Gird, businessman, engineer, and miner
AUTHOR'S COLLECTION

After a few roundups it became apparent that mysterious losses almost equaled the number of new calves. The owners had decided not to use American cowboys on the ranch, due to the strong feelings between Mexican vaqueros and American cowboys. Since they shipped all salable cattle to the United States, and most supplies came from Tombstone, the Mexicans considered the ranch an American company; therefore, it wasn't any sin to steal from them.

M. M. O'Gorman, who with Dick Gird owned the California and Mexican Land and Cattle Company, handled the situation brilliantly. He went to Colonel Emilio Kosterlitzsky, the commander of the Mexican Rurales in Sonora, and bluntly asked, "Colonel, may I ask what your pay is in the Mexican Army?" The Colonel told him. "Colonel I am putting you down on my payroll for the same amount," stated O'Gorman. Thus was started one of the oddest and most famous partnerships along the border.

A Mexican colonel's pay was not very much in American money; the cost to O'Gorman was slight. Under Kosterlitzsky's guardianship, huge trainloads of cattle went to Chino for fattening up on the waste sugar pulp from the mill, which up to that time was a total loss. Wily O'Gorman was a hard man to defeat.

When the Americans imposed a tariff of five to ten dollars per head on foreign cattle, an act that would have bankrupted the cattleman, O'Gorman bought a small ranch along the American–Mexican border, on the American side. Border fences did not exist, and cattle in both countries had the same brand. It was amazing the vast number of cattle that came from that little American ranch.

Cattle Drives in the Old West

During roundup, Mark Hicks started gathering cattle at his ranch and worked the land up to the Salt River. This was a co-op drive with everyone in the area participating. One rancher would meet with another cattle-man and his herd, and the two would join their stock. Every ranch had its brand and mark, so ownership was easily established. This newly formed herd would join another big bunch. The process would continue until all the cattle going to market were contained in one big herd.

Once they had gathered the herd, they headed out on the trail to the market, or shipping point, which was usually Holbrook, although some of the drives were to Wilcox, Mesa, Geronimo, or Fort Thomas. At the market they met up with the cattle buyers and the government inspectors, who checked the cattle and the brands.

It took twenty to twenty-five punchers to handle a herd of five hundred to one thousand head. These drovers needed to be constantly on the alert to keep the herd moving and to protect the cows from rustlers, Indi-ans, and wild animals. Usually the foreman of the drive—or the owner of most of the cattle—led off from the riding point, or pointed the way for the herd to travel. Men would ride on each side of the herd to keep them bunched and to prevent any unruly stock from turning back or drifting off to one side. The largest group of men rode drag at the rear of the herd to keep them moving. At the start of the drive, it was quite a job to stop the cattle from turning back to their home pastures.

How the drive progressed depended in part on the condition of the cattle. When the cattle were fat in a season with plenty of rain and good graze, they stepped along lively, causing the punchers to ride hard after them to keep them bunched. When the cattle were weak from poor grazing, they needed pushing, and the whole herd moved slowly and required a great deal of persuading. When the cattle were poor, they were easier to handle at night; they were willing to bed down and stay down until morning.

The camp wagon with the grub for the men, extra saddles, equipment, and extra feed for the horses that were used the most went ahead of the herd. It was the job of the grub-wagon driver to figure out where the herd would be at night so he could make camp and have supper ready when the drive got there. The stopping place needed to have good water and a resting ground where there was some graze for the cattle so they could fill up before bedding down for the night. The frequently used trails were like cattle highways, with water supplies and safe bedding areas well established.

If the grub-wagon driver was going slower than usual, he did not make it to the camp that night. When that happened, the men didn't get any supper, and the cattle and horses received no water until the next morning when everyone arrived at the assigned spot. When the driver finally joined the herd, some very discontented cowboys, making no bones about their unhappiness, greeted him. In these cases the men got supper and breakfast at the same time. Drovers got only the two meals a day. The first meal was in the morning before they mounted up to continue the drive; the second meal was at night just before they bedded down.

At night, herders rode around the cattle to keep them from drifting and spooking. The night duties were in two or three shifts so that all the men got some sleep, and everyone got assigned night work.

A ramada accompanied every drive. These were the extra horses. No horse could carry a puncher doing the running, and dodging that was necessary for the job for more than a few hours at a time, certainly not for more than half a day. Each puncher had his personal string. These were mounts that either he picked out or were assigned to him at the beginning of the drive. Punchers took pride in their string and were responsible for shoeing their horses and taking caring of them on the trail.

Sometimes the drovers had little choice in their rides, and Joe Winsor was a bit shaky when the foreman of the Flying H Ranch roped out a little hogback horse for him. Winsor let him out, and under the cottonwood tree, he threw him down and shod him. The next morning, when they started out on the roundup, he saddled up his horse and it began bucking. He held on, preferring to fight the ride than hit the ground, although his hands did hit the ground two or three times. He hung tough and broke that horse, causing one of the onlookers to comment, "That Mormon kid is no handsome rider, but he sure holds on."

The Flying H Ranch had a bunch of wild horses on the drive. Someone had a contract to break them, but only succeeded halfway. Winsor made a deal with a Mexican broncobuster. They would help each other with their horses. This deal worked out so well that the foreman gave the two of them that bunch of wild horses to tame.

For this roundup, a thousand head of steer took to the trail and headed for the nearest railroad town. One or two punchers handled the ramada. On a big drive, the ramada could number as many as 150 horses. Each puncher was usually given six horses for his string when driving in dry weather and feeding the horses grain. When the natural grass was good, a puncher had as many as eight mounts assigned to him so that all the horses had time to graze.

The horse herd either followed the cattle, or ran just ahead of them. That made them easily available any time of day. When a puncher needed a fresh horse, he rode up to the ramada, roped and saddled one of his string, then turned his tired mount loose to join the ramada.

A cattle drive following another one would pick up the stray cattle from the preceding herd and bring them in with their cows. If the buyer did not recognize the brand of the stray, he wrote a check for the herd he was buying and took the strays along with them. The buyer would then advertise for the unknown owners in available newspapers. When an owner answered the advertisement, the buyer sent him a check.

Once at the shipping pens it was often difficult to get cars in fast enough to take care of the herds. It was not unusual to find the pens filled when a cattle drive arrive. When that happened, it was necessary to find nearby holding pens for the excess stock until a pen or shipping car was available at the track.

Cattlemen could not reserve cars, because they never knew when their stock would arrive at the shopping point. There were cases when the cattle were on hold for as long as three weeks waiting for a free car. At the shipping pens cattle buyers took over the herd, wrote out a check for the owners, and set the punchers loose. After a long season on the range, topped off with a two-month duty drive, the punchers were dry and ready to quench their thirst. That kept the railroad towns booming day and night

Drovers, like Tom Wills, had to be always alert for stampedes on cattle drives. In 1869 he took a herd of cattle to New Mexico for the old Aleman Ranch. There were eleven hundred head in the herd, all cows, which were easy to handle and not likely to stampede. Wills explained the problems:

It's different with a herd of bulls, a flash of a match, a stamping of boots, even shaking the saddle will send them off. There is always a leader, and he will just run and the cows will follow him. He needs to be turned, and the herd will follow.

When cattle are alarmed in country that is unfamiliar to them, especially at night, they quickly become panicky. They high tail it away from the racket that has disturbed them, and they do it fast, in less than two minutes a puncher can lose sight of a whole herd.

Night herders have to ride around cattle at night to keep them from drifting and spooking. Sometimes when driving fat cattle, the herd will stampede every night for several nights in succession, than all hands have to turn out and chase them, bunch them up again, and stay with them until they get quiet and bedded down. Cowboys would often sing to the herd after a stampede to quiet them down. Fortunately, not that many cattle were lost from stampedes. A few were crippled, and sometimes fifteen to twenty head got away, but a following trail drive would pick them up.

The independent rancher owners did not hire many punchers, but they did pay the same wages as the big ranches. Most of the punchers had no preference of whom they worked for, but when looking for a riding job, they would hit the big outfits first. Since they hired more men, chances were greater that there would be a job open.

WORKING ALONE

For the cattleman just starting out, ranching could be a lonesome life. Most could not afford to hire a bunch of punchers, and they usually worked their ranches with the help of their wife and one or two cowboys. Because the work was dangerous, it had to be scheduled and shared as much as possible. Jack Durham knew that, yet on October 10, 1916, he decided to go alone after a bunch of saddle horses that had gone up the mountain.

On the trail, his horse made a misstep and fell. Horse and rider rolled down the mountainside. The horse got up and ran away, leaving Durham on the ground with a broken leg. It was around two o'clock in the afternoon, and he knew if he did not start for home, no one would ever find him.

The hardest thing for him was to begin on the first mile down the mountain even though the pain and misery increased from then on. He was convinced he better crawl or die right there. He walked on his knees, dragging his broken leg the first few miles. He started out with a pair of chaps and a pair of gloves. He wore down the chaps and had to use the worn gloves for his knees. That left his hands unprotected. Durham's hands were soon covered with cholla needles.

The last two miles of crawling damaged his knees so bad he couldn't get down on them for two years. He almost gave out a half a mile from home, and it was only the thought that he and his wife were never apart without him telling her where he was that kept him going. He crawled about sixty miles through brush, rocks, and gopher holes, and barely managed to avoid a rattlesnake nest. The horse arrived home the next morning, but Durham didn't get home until sunup the following day. His wife went nearly crazy waiting for him.

He was almost dead for lack of water. The thought of it was just heaven, and he was spitting cotton until he could spit no more. He tried to roll a cigarette, but his hands were too cold. Lily put water to boil and washed out his leg. She picked gravel from his knees for the next two years. She gave him a cup of coffee and a piece of toast and let him sleep for two hours before they headed for the doctor in Florence.

Jack Durham had an advantage over Oscar Buckalew: He had a wife as a working partner. In the beginning, Buckalew had a wife working with him on his ranch. Then she discovered ranch life was not to her liking. She left him in 1900 and headed back to Pennsylvania, where she quickly obtained a divorce. Shortly after the divorce, Buckalew moved onto a ranch in Helvetia and started raising stock.

Ranch life became too lonely for him, and he advertised in the papers back East for a wife. He declared himself a young man, hoping that the woman would find out how young he was in spirit. At the time he was fifty-seven years old. A twenty-year-old woman answered his advertisement. They corresponded, and decided that two young people in love ought to get married.

Buckalew arranged to meet his mail-order bride in Vail. When the train pulled up at the station, the young, sweet thing stepped down and searched for the dashing young man who would carry her away to his ranch. When she met her husband-to-be, she became unreasonable, she wouldn't even give him the chance to prove that a man is as young as he feels. She made it quite clear that she would not marry him under any circumstances, youthful feeling be damned.

Working the Ranch

When cattle grazed in mountain areas, Tom Wills discovered they multiplied faster. However, no lone vaquero could tackle a three- or four-year-old wild cow. Rounding them up was difficult and dangerous and required skill, and sometimes subterfuge.

Wills knew tame cattle would go wild when let loose among the wild herd, so he figured he could tame wild cattle by mixing them with a domestic herd. He hoped the wild cattle would follow the domestic herd into the corral, where the punchers could burn their brand and mark their ears.

He took tame cattle up into the canyons and drove the wild cattle toward them, letting them all mill around and mix. The wild one-year-olds easily followed the tame cattle, but the old ones were a hard proposition. Finally the punchers lassoed the stubborn oldsters, tied their horns to trees with just enough room for them to move around the trunk, and left them there for three days. Eventually these tough steers realized that resistance was futile. After the three days, they joined with the tame cattle for feed and were manageable. The horns on the wild cattle, which could do considerable damage, were sawed off before the animals were let loose.

In the old days, Albert West never branded at a chute. The branding of calves took place out on the range. Unbranded calves, missed on the range, got their brands in the corral at roundup time. There were no fences on the ranges, and the corrals were the only enclosures for holding the cattle.

For range branding, the puncher carried a branding iron on his saddle. When he saw an unbranded maverick calf on the range, he would rope the critter, tie all four feet together, make a small fire, heat his branding iron, and stamp it on the calf. Of course, the calf's mother often offered strenuous objections at the treatment of her bawling baby.

Branding in the corral was much easier, and faster. Cowboys herded mavericks into the big corral, then built up a good fire and heated several irons at one time. Some punchers roped and dragged the calves to the fire; others held them while a hot iron slapped their hides, branding them. After branding, the calves scampered into the herd, or returned to their mothers, loudly complaining about their disrespectful treatment.

A DIFFERENT RANCH

Not all of the ranches in the Old West raised cattle. A few raised sheep, that avowed enemy of the cattle industry. While cattlemen and sheep raisers did not make for good neighbors, the animosity was not as virulent as claimed. Although they avoided each other as much as possible, there was plenty of free land in the old days to allow enough acreage for everyone.

Stories fill Westerns about cattle and sheep conflicts. Some of these stories of range wars were more fiction than fact. Although when flocks of sheep started grazing on public land, and many cattlemen saw the amount of their available graze land disappearing, this caused discontent to escalate into violence. From Wyoming to Texas and from Oregon to Colorado, there were reports of "range wars."

Arizona had its share of conflicts, murder, and the slaughter of flocks. The most famous one was the Tewksbury–Graham feud, which ironically started two years before the Tewksburys introduced sheep onto their land. The feud initially had nothing to do with the cattle–sheep issue. An original motivating factor in the animosity was racism. For the most part, sheep owners were Hispanic or Native American; cattlemen were American (European derivative).

Reports of sheep ruining the graze land by chopping too close, or softening the earth, are partially untrue. Blame for the destruction of much of the Old West's grazing land is the fault of old-time ranchers who grazed too many cattle and took poor care of the land. Today, with proper land management, ranchers are raising sheep and cattle together on their land.

Warren Allison and his family brought sheep into Arizona in the late fall of 1874. The drive started in San Diego and met with all sorts of misfortune. Some of the sheep ate Loco Weed and went crazy. The Allisons had to leave them there beside the road. When they reached water, they had to get ahead of the flock to scatter them. If any mired in the mud, those behind would jump on top of them and trample them to death. During the night it was necessary to guard the sheep from the roving bands of coyotes that plagued the flock.

When the Allisons reached the Colorado River, about thirty miles below Yuma, it was raining hard and Hualapai Smith, the ferryman, refused to run the ferry. They had to hire Indians to help them cross the river. At first the sheep refused to get into the boat. When they finally were able to get them aboard, they loaded too many and the ferry started to sink. They reduced the load and tied several to the back end of the boat.

While crossing, the Yuma Indians waded into the river and pulled the boat diagonally across part of the way. When the water became deep, the Indians jumped into the boat and with long poles pushed the boat for thirty or forty feet across the deepest part. That night they let the sheep run loose. But it turned cold that night, and about seventy-five of the sheep froze to death.

Leaving the sheep in the care of his siblings and his mother, Allison and his father headed back to the mountains in San Diego, where they had left the balance of the sheep. While they were gone, the Indians tried to run off some small bands of sheep, but Charles Allison, who was guarding the flock, shot at them, chasing them off.

The trip back to Yuma went much quicker for them, as they were traveling on a familiar road and knew where to find water. Reaching their Colorado River camp, they rested while a team went into Yuma for provisions.

Sticking to the Overland stage road, they followed the Gila River. Recent rains made good graze for them all the way to Tucson. Still, the last part of the trip was not easy. From Gila Bend to Casa Grande, they traveled forty-five miles without freshwater. Along the route they found a pool of alkali water and had to guard the sheep to keep them away from it.

Finally arriving in Tucson in March 1875, the Allison family stocked up at the Tully and Ochoa store on Main Street before leaving for their new home in Calabasas. Tucson merchants Pinckney Tully and Estevan Ochoa at one time kept a bunch of Mexican sheep at Calabasas. They built a good corral there, which was now abandoned. It was ideal for the Allisons, who took it over. The boys took care of the sheep, and corralled them every night. The corral was about a quarter of a mile west of the house, and the wild animals, mountain lions, wolves, and coyotes, were so plentiful that a guard had to sleep in the corral.

One night a lion jumped into the corral and killed a sheep. The Allisons managed to run the lion out before he could eat any part of the sheep, then they put strychnine in the carcass and left it where the lion had killed it. The second night the lion came back and ate his fill. He died in the corral. Another night a pack of wolves got into the corral and killed eleven sheep before the guards ran them out of the corral.

During sheering season, the Allisons packed the fleece in huge woolsacks and delivered it to Tully and Ochoa in Tucson. The freighters used big wagons pulled by oxen and mule teams and hauled the wool to La Junta, Colorado, six hundred miles away. From there the wool went to factories in Philadelphia, Pennsylvania.

The next spring the Apache Indians went up to the top of a high peak in the San Cayatano Mountains, a spot that gave them a view a long way up and down the Santa Cruz Valley. Spotting the Allison herds, they went down during the night and stole all the working animals. That fall the grass seed ripened, producing two kinds of pin grass seed. The seeds got into the wool of the sheep and worked through the hide, between the hide and the flesh, causing the sheep to scratch and rub all their wool off. That was the end of the Allisons' sheep business. They sold the ranch and part of the sheep flock to a man by the name of Mott.

The Allisons were not the only pioneers to try their hand at sheep. North of Tucson, prospector Alexander McKay decided to raise sheep. In 1882 he bought some from Mr. Hilton, out beyond Pantano, and started a ranch about a mile northwest of his house in Oracle. The gamma grass was knee-high all over the country, and it was not hard to care for the sheep. He put Maxwell Bruce to work herding while he continued to prospect.

McKay collaborated with W. C. Davis, and they started out with four hundred sheep. They bought an additional sixty-five hundred from Sanford. McKay didn't intend to go into the sheep business, but he was having some problems with one of his mines. While working the Christmas Mine, he would get into a rich spot, then a bare spot. One day he told Maxwell Bruce to put a shot into the hanging wall. He did, and with it tapped into an underground stream. The water came up so fast they could no longer work the mine.

McKay built a house on the mesa, put in four and half miles of pipe, and built a rock corral to hold the sheep. The lions, bears, coyotes, foxes, and badgers constantly troubled them. A badger could catch a young lamb by the throat and hold on until it was dead. One night a lion got into the corral, grabbed one of the biggest sheep, and jumped over the rock wall. The next morning McKay and Bruce followed the blood and found the carcass. Knowing that once lions make a kill, they feast on the carcass for several days, they poisoned what was left of the dead sheep. The lion went back to feed and died from the poison.

RIDING WITH THE HASHKNIFE

The life of the "professional" wrangler who worked the big ranches presented a different scenario than that of the cowboy who worked for the small independent rancher. The big outfits required different skills, prizing not the man who could handle cattle, but the one who was expert with a six shooter and handy with a branding iron. This job description attracted mostly men who were ruthless, cruel, and temperamental with low morals. Killing and gunfighting were part of their life and ways.

During the 1880s, Arizona was home to large ranches that had some of the roughest, most unconscionable punchers working for them. The Aztec Land and Cattle Company, better known as *the* Hashknife for its brand, was such an outfit. The punchers were outlaws, men hiding out, drifters, and runaways.

Claude Nichols was under ten when he ran away on a stolen horse—armed with a stolen gun—from a brutal father in Texas. On the fourth day of his escape, he finished the last of his rations and was miles from any sign of human habitation. At that point he was so discouraged he didn't know or care what might become of him. When he ran across fresh tracks of a trail herd, he wasn't sure if he would find Indians or white rustlers; he didn't care, and he had to have food.

It was getting dark when he rode into the trail camp, which had about five thousand head of Texas longhorns. He had no idea whose cattle they were. All he wanted was something to eat. No one paid any attention to him, treating him much like a stray dog that had wandered in. The hands were eating supper around the campfire. Nichols dismounted, walked over by the cook wagon, and stood there waiting for somebody to say something to him. The cook didn't say a word; he just filled up a tin plate and handed it to the boy. It didn't take the kid long to finish the food.

Nichols figured out who the big boss was and tried to keep his eyes on him. He was a mean-looking man and made shivers run up the boy's back. Although he knew all of the men had seen him, none of them even looked at him, except the cook.

When he finished eating, he washed his plate and cup as he had seen the others do, then got up enough nerve to ask the cook if he could roll his bed down for the night. The cook told him to bed down by the chuck wagon, remarking, "Sort of hungry wasn't you kid?" Nichols admitted it was good grub, and then he asked whose outfit it was.

"Now kid, don't go askin' questions, just go to sleep and I'll give you 'nother feed in the mornin' . . . you see kid, Boss McIntire don't like questions."

Boss McIntire! That name gave Nichols the chills. He had heard that name before, but had never seen the man. His pa and Uncle Jim mentioned that name with plenty of cuss words. He was scared out of his wits, but because he was dead tired and groggy from so much food, he went right off to sleep and didn't wake up until the cook called him the next morning. He rustled firewood for the cook and helped him get breakfast ready. Boss McIntire got his plate and sat down by the boy, but acted as if he hadn't seen him. The kid squirmed as if ants were crawling all over him.

After breakfast Nichols started to saddle up with the punchers. He didn't look over nine years old, and it was about all he could do to lift the heavy old saddle onto his horse's back. As he hefted it up, he looked over at Boss McIntire and caught him looking him over.

"Stray in the herd this mornin' boys, what'll we do with it?" he said to the others.

"Aw don't kill it Boss, it ain't fat 'nuff to eat," pronounced one of the cowhands.

Turning to the young man, Boss McIntire asked, "Whose kid are yuh? Where's you come from?"

The boy straighten up, "Name's Claude Nichols. Came from nowhere," was the only answer he could come up with, fear making him pale around the gills. McIntire roared out, "Smart ain't yuh! What in hell yuh doin' here anyhow?"

"Nuthin'," stammered the kid.

"Nuthin' eh? Well kid, people don't just do nuthin' around this outfit. Nichols? Hump. Any kin to Jim Nichols? He send you out here?"

The boy turned even paler; he knew from what his pa and Uncle Jim said that Boss McIntire was the man who had caused Uncle Jim to go to the pen. He wasn't going to be a coward, and he answered back, "Listen mister, I don't care what yuh done to my Uncle Jim, I don't care if he did go to the Pen, or who sent him there, he oughta be there now I allow. I ain't gonna go back where I come from. He didn't send me here, and yuh can't make me go back either."

With that the pint-size cowboy jerked an old rusty .45 out of his saddlebag and threatened to shoot himself; he wasn't going to be forced back home, and he wasn't going to let any of that bunch beat him up or maybe kill him. McIntire jerked the gun out of the boy's hands and slapped his head half off.

"Them damn things is dangerous for boys your size son. Who the hell said yuh had to go back?" The friendly tone of his voice relaxed the boy.

"Know anything about wrangling hosses, or punching cattle?" asked McIntire.

Nichols was feeling braver by the minute, "I don't know nuthin' 'bout nuthin, 'septin' a hoss whip, a plow, 'n a cotton hoe, but I reckon I could learn most anything if yuh could give me a job."

McIntire looked that kid straight in the eye for several minutes. "Where's yore Uncle Jim now?" he wanted to know.

That didn't set well with the kid, who was feeling a bit queasy by McIntire's attention. However, he was determined to act brave. "He was stealin' hosses with the Rangers ridin' his tail, the last I heard of him, way last spring, over a year I reckon." Boss McIntire suspected the boy was telling the truth, for he grinned, and said he would give this Nichols kid a job if he wanted to go to New Mexico.

For the next ten years, Claude Nichols wrangled for the Hashknife outfit. He worked for them in New Mexico, and with Pete Brogden in Arizona on the Hashknife horse ranch at Garland, near Williams. He also worked on the headquarters ranch near Holbrook.

Boss McIntire was as crooked as a barrel of snakes, and he knew more about brands than any man who lived. Human life was no more to him than a dog or coyote, but he always shot square with his men, and always paid them what he said he would.

The first time Claude Nichols quit the Hashknife, it was because of Pete Brogden. Brogden was one of McIntire's pets. He had been with him since he was a little shaver, joining the Hashknife outfit when he was about seven. They said Brogden was a man bullets wouldn't kill. Although shot several times, he always recovered. All the men were jealous of Brogden, and he was jealous of Nichols. His fear was that this tyke would take over his place in McIntire's esteem.

Brogden and Nichols were bound to clash. It came over a horse. McIntire gave Nichols, a horse that Brogden wanted, and he took after Nichols to get it. The older man got the best of the fifteen-year-old kid in the fight, and Nichols tried to shoot him, swore he would do it someday. However, George Beasly, one of the punchers in the outfit, yanked the gun away from the teen. Beasly didn't like Brogden either, but he didn't want Nichols to get in bad with Boss McIntire. The next morning Nichols and Beasly rode out and worked together most of the day.

When the wranglers came in that night, Brogden was missing. While they were eating supper, his hoss came in riderless with blood on the saddle. McIntire heard about the fight between Nichols and Brogden and asked the young hand if he had shot Pete.

Beasly stuck up for the kid. He said he had ridden with him all that day, and he had his gun. However, it was obvious the whole bunch thought he had done it. A search party found Brogden shot up and unconscious from loss of blood. Boss McIntire acted as if Pete might have been his own son; he broke down and cried like a woman.

Nichols thought he better move on and head for healthier places. When McIntire paid off Nichols, he told him, "Kid I hope you don't get too danged handy with that gun, might wind up like yourn Uncle Jim did. I shore hate to see that, Kid. Pete won't die; bullets can't kill Pete, but it's hell to see him suffer like that." Nichols left wondering just which one of the boys actually did shoot Pete.

Claude Nichols headed out for Montana and got a job punching cattle for the Diamond A Ranch near Helena. He stayed there less than six months. He got in a jam over a card game with a fellow named Bob Smith, and he left before he found out if he killed him. Fortunately he didn't. He came back to Arizona and went to work for Toles Cosper on the Blue Range. When he got tired of that job, he headed out for Flagstaff, and that's where he ran into Boss McIntire again and decided to go back to work for the Hashknife. McIntire figured the best way to patch up the feelings between Nichols and Brogden was to have the young cowboy work for Brogden.

Nichols was at the home ranch when a gang of Mexican rustlers tried to get off with some of the Hashknife horses. Nichols, Brogden,

Beasly, and two other cowboys went after them and ran them down where they were camped in a little basin. The Hashknife boys strung them up in a tree.

Shortly after the hanging, some of the Hashknife boys rode with Commodore Owen's posse, looking for those culprits who "strung up the rustlers." Three members of that posse were Beasly, Brogden, and Nichols. When one of the dogs found Brogden's watch at the place where the rustlers died, the Hashknife boys thought that was the end for them. Somehow, although they never knew how, they got out of that jam. Boss McIntire had a way of getting his men out of trouble.

Claude Nichols left the Hashknife and took a job with Bood Brookin on the Double Circle Ranch, another big outfit where being handy with a six shooter was more important than knowing about cattle.

Pete Brogden lived to be around ninety years old. He died in an automobile accident in Clarksdale, Arizona, in 1933. After he died, they found around ninety bullet wounds in his body, and about seventy-six knife wounds. He was a man that bullets couldn't kill.

William Thomas Sanders was another young man who found himself involved with the Hashknife, although he came to them from a circuitous route. He left Texas when he was seventeen, looking for work and chasing the rumors about the wild Arizona Territory. He and his pal Jasper Jones had no money or means of transportation. They saddled up a couple of stray horses that were hanging around the neighborhood, and didn't bother about ownership.

They worked with different cow outfits for two or three months, trying to get a grubstake as they went along. They kept moving in the direction of Arizona. They landed in Flagstaff in the spring of 1878. There were plenty of tough outfits around Flagstaff: the Hashknife, the Pine Tree, and the Yellowjackets. They all employed a nondescript crew of tough gunslingers. One didn't have to know a cow from an elephant to get a job with them. Wranglers had to be a gunslinger first, and had to be smart enough to keep out of the way of the other gangs.

In Flagstaff, Sanders met Pete Brogden, who now was the foreman of the Hashknife outfit on Garland Prairie. Brogden was also a Texas stray, and perhaps because of that he felt protective of Sanders. He wouldn't

Wranglers on the Aztec Land and Cattle Company, aka The Hashknife
NATIONAL ARCHIVES

give Sanders a job. He told him he hated to see him get mixed up with his gang.

Sanders landed a job with Babbit Brothers. The cook went on a bender and quit. Sanders was hired on as cook, although he knew nothing about the art of whipping up meals for punchers. First thing he did was cook a twenty-five-pound box of dried apples. When he discovered he didn't have enough pots, he began digging holes and hiding apples so the boss wouldn't see them. When the men arrived for dinner, all they had to eat were dried apples. That ended Sanders's cooking career. The boss put him to riding the range, and that's what he did for two years.

When he quit Babbit Brothers, he went over to Prescott and helped lay the first railroad track between Ashfork and Prescott. Just as that job finished, he met Albert Blevins, the brother of Andy Cooper, who was a notorious gunslinger. Cooper was involved in the Tonto Basin War. Blevins was right handy with a running iron. He introduced Sanders to

Boss McIntire, and Sanders went to Holbrook, finally working for the Hashknife on their headquarters cattle ranch.

When the Tonto Basin War broke out, Sanders decided that he preferred riding with a whole skin rather than letting his neck stretch a rope. He left the Hashknife outfit, riding fast. The Hashknife cured him of his wild ways, and he married Phoebe Freeman in 1892. He started his own successful ranch near the Gila River in Duncan Valley.

TROUBLE ON THE DOUBLE CIRCLE

Claude Nichols found himself a hand at the Double Circle when the Tonto Basin War broke out. Although he was not involved in it, he did know most of the fellows who were. It was in 1898 when he signed on with the Double Circle. That outfit could always use a man who was handy with a six shooter or running iron. Brookin's operations were shady, but then most of the big outfits were somewhat suspect.

The Double Circle had just taken on two new hands, Seth and Ben Bedford from Texas. Bood Brookin swore he didn't know them; he said he hired them in Clifton because he needed a couple of extra men for spring roundup. Turns out, he did know them, and so did Jink Williamson and Joe Boyd, a couple of punchers working for the outfit at the time. They were from Texas, as was most of the outfit.

The foreman lied when he said those two boys were looking for a job when he met them in Clifton. What they needed was a good hideout. When they arrived at the Double Circle, Nichols saw them unload their saddlebags full of long green and stack them in the ranch safe.

Apparently, someone in Bood Brookin's outfit saw a good chance to get all that loot and tipped off the rangers. The Texas Rangers had followed a trail that turned cold in Clifton, and they never would have gotten any farther without the tip. The lawmen mounted a posse in Clifton and rode straight to the ranch. It was in the afternoon, almost quitting time, and the wranglers had been peeling broncos all day in the home corral. All the riders except the Bedfords were unarmed.

Claude Nichols had just finished riding and was sitting on the corral fence trying to catch his breath. The other boys were blindfolding another bronco, getting the horse ready for the saddle. Williamson and Boyd went into the house. It turned out they were after their guns, although no one knew it at the time. It seems they were expecting the rangers.

The Bedford boys were standing outside the corral facing the house when the posse showed up. It looked like there were fifty riders in that posse, but in reality it was only about twenty. The riders circled around the corral and barn, scattered, and without a word began shooting at the Bedfords. The Bedford Brothers started shooting back, and the gunfight was on.

Looking for a safe place, Nichols reached for a tall pine right by the fence and quickly began to climb. Just as he got halfway up that pine, a bullet hit the tree not two inches from his head. He looked around and saw both Williamson and Boyd at the corner of the barn. One of them had fired that shot at him.

Just then, Seth took a bullet in the wrist and dropped his gun. He said something to Ben. Ben kept shooting. He hit one of the rangers and one of the other men in the posse. Then Nichols saw Williamson take aim at Seth Bradford, and Boyd take aim at the other brother. The rest of the boys had scurried away as soon as the shooting started. Everything ended when both Bradfords fell. At the end of the shootout, there were four dead men and eight wounded.

As soon as Nichols realized he was a target, he figured he had found out too much to suit the Double Circle bunch, and to stay healthy he needed to leave. He slid down that tree, grabbed one of the snubbing horses, and left for Toles Cosper's ranch. Cosper managed to find out what happened after Nichols left. The posse rolled the Bradford Brothers in their blankets and buried them where they fell. Brookin swore he didn't know anything about the brothers and their money, and he managed to convince the law. The general opinion was that the Bedfords had stashed the swag some place before they came out to the Double Circle.

Bood Brookin claimed the shootout broke him flat and caused him to leave the country. A few days later, Nichols ran into Williamson and Boyd in a gambling dive in Clifton. They carried rolls that would have chocked a cow. They claimed they won it all in a high-stake poker game. They left for Texas right after that. Williamson came back to Arizona some years later, a broken old man. He died of heart trouble.

James V. Parks was also at the Double Circle when the Bedford brothers' killings occurred. His perspective was different from Nichols. He rode in with the posse. Parks wore a lawman's badge most of his life. In the 1890s he was a deputy for A. A. Anderson when Anderson was sheriff of Graham County.

He remembered the two Texas Rangers that rode into the county looking for a pair of Texas train robbers. Parks was in Clifton the day the rangers got the tip that their men were out at the Double Circle Ranch. He, the sheriff, and the rangers joined the posse that went out to the Double Circle. They got to the ranch about sundown and found the Bedford boys busting broncos in the home corral. One of them was initially unarmed. They were tough to take as it was, but it would have been a lot more difficult if both outlaws initially had guns when the lawmen arrived. The brothers were no cowards, and as it was the posse did not get off without bloodshed.

It was difficult to say who shot the Bedfords, for everyone was shooting at the same time. Bood Brookin and two of his men came out of the house shooting at the outlaws as soon as the pose opened fire. Maybe Brookin was trying to defend himself for harboring the outlaws.

They buried the bodies at the ranch that night, not taking time to make a coffin for them. The posse had two of its own dead, and one man wounded, and needed to get back to town to look after their casualties.

The robbers were supposed to have their loot from the train robbery with them. However, Bood Brookin denied any knowledge of it. The law needed proof before it could do anything with a man, whether he was lying or not. As far as the law knew, the loot never turned up.

The law arrested Brookin and accused him of hiding the train robbers; somehow he managed to get clear. Although he claimed the incident broke him, a few months after his release from jail, he bought a herd of one thousand cattle from Bug Ming—and he paid seven thousand dollars in cash for them.

About three months later the two Bell Brothers, who were helping the Double Circle outfit with the roundup when the train robbers showed up, were found shot to death over on Eagle Creek, their bodies riddled with bullets; no clue was ever found as to who did it, or what for.

An Honest Start

The Double Circle did not start out as an outfit of outlaws and gunslingers. It started out like most Arizona's early ranches: as a one-man, one-family operation. At the Double Circle, that man was George Stevens.

In the spring of 1872, Stevens settled on his homestead section of 640 acres that bordered the eastern line of the San Carlos Indian Reservation. He built a cabin and then returned to Silver City to drive his stock to his new ranch. His herd was twenty-five nondescript breed cows and one longhorn bull. He paid twenty-five dollars for the bull and called it Tex Southerland after the former owner. Stevens knew the bull was from a herd stolen around Seven Rivers, New Mexico, but that was a long way away and had nothing to do with him.

Stevens and his herd arrived on the ranch on May 7. That herd was plagued with problems from the beginning. In the first few months, Indians and anyone else who wanted beef helped themselves to a critter they found out on the range, regardless of its brand. The Indians figured that as long as cattle were near the reservation, or their hunting ground, it was their right to take it.

On the night of November 3, 1874, while Mr. and Mrs. Stevens were in Clifton buying winter supplies, the Apaches raided and burned their ranch house. Pedro Baca, the Stevens's vaquero, received an arrow wound in his left shoulder, yet managed to escape and make it to one of the mining camps in Metcalf Canyon, where his wound was treated. Charlie Metcalf rode into town to report the disaster to the Stevens.

Stevens left his family in town that winter while he attended to his mining claims. As soon as the snows melted, he went back to the ranch, rebuilt his cabin, and moved his family back home. He found a few of his old range cows and their calves near the ranch. Stevens rounded them up with the help of a newly hired cowboy and Pedro Baca. He instructed his hands to guard them, and if any Indians came across the creek to kill a beef, they were to shoot to kill.

In the spring of 1877, the Double Circle brand went on fifty spring calves. Stevens also branded and broke twenty-five horses. The ranch house had a couple of rooms added to it, and new barns and corrals were constructed. On the morning of August 15, 1877, Mrs. Stevens was alone with her two small children. At the sound of hooves, she went to the door. Pedro Baca rode up to the ranch house and fell off his horse at her feet. He was mortally wounded, but managed to gasp out, "Indians kill Juan Ortega . . . take cattle . . . come here . . . run."

The tough and determined pioneer woman got the buckboard ready, loaded in some household things and any food she could quickly grab, put the children in the wagon, loaded her rifle, and started for safety on the only trail to the mining camp. It was thirty-five miles distance on what was scarcely more than an unbroken horse trail. She fervently hoped she might meet some roving prospector.

It was midmorning when she started out. She didn't know if she and the children would reach safety. If her husband reached the ranch, he would see destruction and find his family missing. She could not go to his mining claims to warn him, as the Indians were in that direction.

Near daybreak the following morning, the exhausted wife arrived in the Metcalf mining camp and spread the alarm. A posse of armed men started out in search of George Stevens. When they reached the ranch, they found a charred ruin. They followed the trail left by the Indians on to the reservation and met George riding a wounded horse. They gladly delivered the news about the safety of his family.

The evening before, Stevens had returned to the ranch, unaware of the Indian outbreak, and found his house a blazing ruin and his family missing. When he spied the body of Pedro Baca, he knew that the Indians were to blame and his family was either dead or captive. He followed the trail of the raiders onto the reservation. When his horse sustained an arrow wound, he turned back to the mining camp intending to call out the soldiers from the fort.

The authorities questioned Chief Geronimo about the killing of the two Mexican ranch hands, the destruction of the ranch, and the stealing of the branded herd. His braves were skinning a beef on the reservation, he explained, and the Mexicans interfered. He denied knowing anything about the cattle or the burning of the ranch house.

Stevens refused to be undone. He did not have a hoof or a horn or a roof left. His old bull, Tex Sutherland, was gone with the rest of the herd. All he had left was one saddle horse. He defiantly rebuilt his house and moved his family home, again. He hired three men, took a pack outfit, and headed toward the Mexico border to gather a herd and restock his range.

He arrived home in the middle of August 1878 with a herd of three hundred branded cattle and about one hundred unbroken horses that needed branding. Stevens hired eight men who could handle a six-shooter and a branding iron and ordered them to brand any four-legged critter they came across, and to shoot any Indian they found lurking on the range off the reservation.

In the Indian outbreak of 1878, settler Net Tiddon was killed, the Triple X was burned out, and another settler, Mrs. Pippin died on the Triangle T, the Y Bar Y and Double Circle were burned, and most of Stevens's remaining herd was stolen.

In the fall of 1879, a new ranch outfit settled in the area. A man by the name of York from Penasco, New Mexico formed a syndicate with men from Texas and established the C A Bar Ranch. They had a land grant of 640 acres and the availability of plenty of open range. In 1882, a raid destroyed the Purdy Trading Post and the Irish Ranch. The raiders killed two freighters near the trading post, burned their wagons, and killed two C A cowhands. Geronimo's men, wearing war paint, also burned out the Guthrie Ranch and wounded a score of men in a skirmish. The C A Bar syndicate was disgusted, and busted. They decided to dissolve.

Stevens lost more than half of his herd and his horses in the outbreak, but this time the raiders spared his ranch house. Determined to keep going, he purchased seventy-five head of stock from the syndicate. That included five prize Hereford bulls and a few saddle horses.

Shortly after this Indian raid, the railroad built a line along the Gila River that connected the mining district to the main line at Lordsburg, New Mexico. The towns of Duncan, Sheldon, York, and Guthrie sprung up. Shipping facilities were now available, opening up markets to the east, and west to California. Ranchers were optimistic and refused to let the Indians, rustlers, and outlaws chase them out of the territory.

Indians were undaunted by this display of bravado. They wiped out the ranches of Benton Rasberry and the Luther Brothers almost before they got started. They killed Rasberry and one of the Luther Brothers.

They raided the Triple X and other ranches in the area, cleaning them out of stock and burning the houses and barns. Every ranch from the head of the Blue River, down along the San Francisco, and up the Gila to the New Mexico Territory line had their own troubles with Indians and rustlers, but none matched the trials experienced by the ranchers along Eagle Creek bordering the San Carlos Indian Reservation.

They raided Stevens's ranch so often that he had less than one hundred head of cattle and a few saddle horses. He decided he "simply had too many irons in the fire." About this time he struck pay dirt with his mining claims, solving his money problems. Maybe it was time to sell the ranch.

One September 9, 1880, Stevens sold 320 acres of his deeded land and the few cattle and horses he had left to J. H. Hopson and his brother, John for the sum of fifteen hundred dollars. The remaining 320 acres of the homestead belonged to Mrs. Eloise Stevens, his wife, who refused to sell. She leased her acres to R. F. Brooking, known in Texas as Bood Brookin, where he served time for cattle rustling. Mrs. Stevens knew nothing about Brooking's past.

J. H. and John. Hopson also had no knowledge of Brookin's past. To them it would not have mattered. Brookings had the lease on the other half of the Double Circle property, and they needed a ranch manager. They hired him, knowing he intended to run a brand of his own. J. H. Hopson already had a patent on a section joining the original Double Circle property. He leased twenty-five sections across Eagle Creek and added another twenty-five sections south and east of this land. A section is 640 acres. Without fences, the size of his grazing land increased. His cattle could range where they pleased, provided the Indians and rustlers did not find them.

Brookin branded *B Lazy B* on his cattle, and *Muleshoe* on his horses. He established both brands in Texas. However, the only stock he brought to the Arizona Territory with him was his private saddle horse, a roan gilding. The Hopson Brothers ran the Double Circle brand on both cattle and horses.

The Hopson Brothers hired Brookin as the general manager of the Double Circle and left the ranch completely in his hands while they set about buying more cattle. Brookin lived in a shack he built on his leased land. His crew of twenty-seven cowboys occupied the original Double Circle ranch house, rebuilt by the Hopsons.

The Hopsons gathered a herd in Texas of about twenty-five hundred longhorns and Herefords and brought them to the Double Circle ranch, arriving in the middle of June 1890. The Double Circle herds increased by leaps and bounds, although Brookin's herd remained a modest number. The ranchers throughout the country were suspicious and had distrusted Brookin from the beginning. He was handy with a six shooter and a running iron, which was to his credit. However, he was also gruff and had an overbearing manner and a sly snakelike look in his small beady eyes.

In the fall of 1890, George Olney hired four extra men from Texas, known only by their trail names, to help with roundup on the Turtle Ranch. Brookin had some gun talk with the four Turtle hands one Saturday night in the gambling den on Chase Creek in Clifton. A few days later, three of the Turtle hands were found shot to death near their range camp, and the fourth was missing. They rolled the three men in their tarpaulins and buried them where they died in an unmarked grave on the bank of the Black River, just below the head of Fish Creek.

The authorities accused Brookin of the murder, but he denied knowing anything about it, or even knowing the identity of the four Turtle men. At that time the Texas Rangers were in the vicinity looking for four escaped convicts who were doing time for bank robbery. The rangers disappeared about the same time as the killing.

On December 25, 1891, J. H. Hopson gave his brother John T. the Double Circle as a present. The elder Hopson had mining interests that claimed all his attention, leaving him little time to oversee his ranch. In the fall of 1895, Brookin brought in a herd of fifteen hundred cattle from A. Drum and turned them loose on John Hopson's open range. With that, Hopson fired him from his payroll. However, Brookin kept his lease on Mrs. Stevens 320 acres and continued to run his own ranch, right at the back door of the Double Circle.

Brookin still had his personal crew of between nine to fifteen gunmen, every one of them a suspicious character. All his ranch hands were handy with a running iron. While these men were not on the Double

Circle payroll, but on Brookin's, folks still blamed the Double Circle out-fit for the misdeeds in the area.

In 1901, after the Bedford Brothers incident, Brookin sold everything except a saddle horse. He sold his brand and the cattle to H. C. Day, who ran the Lazy B outfit. When he left the Blue Range, he went to Globe. There he established the Fishhook brand, which he eventually sold to a rancher by the name of McGiven. He then bought a service station in Geronimo.

As soon as Brookin cleared out, John Hopson bought the remaining 320 acres of the original Double Circle homestead from the heirs of Elo-ise Stevens. By this time, homesteaders claimed nine of the ten sections of leased section used by the Double Circle to the south and east of the ranch. Hopson found he could not lease any more land off the reservation. His only alternative was to acquire patented homesteads.

Hopson started purchasing the land adjoining his ranch. Steven McCommas sold him 640 acres. From one of the Luther brothers he acquired another 640, and he added two more sections, one from Thomas B. Cook and one from a Mr. Hoffman.

On July 1, 1902, John Hopson sold the Double Circle brand—including six sections that he owned, along with forty-three sections of leased land, and all the cattle and horses—to A. Drum for three hundred thousand dollars. Twenty-four years later, Drum sold one-third interest in the cattle to George Moore. Moore added his homestead section to the Double Circle Land and Cattle Company between 1926 and 1928.

Over the next thirty-five years, the Double Circle changed hands many times and fluctuated in size. A syndicate from Texas bought the Double Circle holdings in 1928. Eight years later, in 1936, D. W. Light bought out the syndicate from the surviving members and heirs. The sale did not include the brand, and an interdict forbade the use of the Double Circle brand in the state of Arizona for ten years. Also in 1936, the gov-ernment withdrew all leased land on the reservations, allowing the cattle ranchers only their deeded land for range purposes, and these had to be under fence. The loss of grazing land could have been a factor in D. W. Light's decision to sell the Double Circle to J. B. Ryan of Globe on Feb-ruary 26, 1937. Ryan kept it only a year, then sold it to Walter R. and C.

Ivan McKinney. Ivan McKinney took charge of the Double Circle, which now had eleven sections of deeded land. On this ranch they raised pure-bred Hereford that needed no brand.

UNDEFEATABLE

Seven miles north of Nogales, on the Santa Cruz River, on a little rocky hill overlooking the surrounding country, Pete Kitchen built his ranch house. He built it of adobe brick, its flat roof surround by a parapet three feet high. In dangerous times Kitchen posted a sentinel to sound the alarm in case of attack. The Indians made incessant raids on the ranch; they killed or drove out his bravest neighbors. They killed his herder, and they slaughtered his stepson, but Pete Kitchen stayed on, and beat them down. His name struck terror in every Apache. In the end, they decided it was wisest to pass him by.

Kitchen came to the Arizona Territory in 1854 from Covington, Kentucky. He lived in Canoa for several years and then moved to a ranch near Nogales called the Protero. He took up a thousand acres of rich bottomland and raised large crops of grain, potatoes, cabbages, and fruit, including melons. He had a large herd of cattle and, his particular delight, a drove of several hundred fine hogs. Knowing Kitchen's pride in the hogs, the Apaches took pleasure in shooting arrows into them, causing them to run squealing to the house looking like porcupines or giant pincushions.

From his pigs, Kitchen produced large quantities of ham and bacon. That was his specialty, and from Nogales to Silver City, New Mexico, store signs announced when *Pete Kitchen Hams* were available. He also supplied the stores with lard and bacon. His estimated income was almost ten thousand dollars a year.

He wasn't an overly large man, standing only about five feet, nine inches. He was spare, erect, and physically fit, even in his old age. His eyes were blue gray and his complexion florid. A quiet man, he was easily recognized by his habitual attire of a broad-brim sombrero and Mexican serape. Kitchen was a man of force, resolution, and general likeability. He was an ideal model of the border man of his day, being brave, friendly, honest, and generous, but he was also profane, a regular drinker, and a constant gambler. For all his faults, and attributes, there is one trait that is unarguable: He was impossible to defeat.

The ranch house, family, and workers at Pete Kitchen's ranch. The large woman at left is probably his wife, and at the left corner of the house is Pete Kitchen.
CHRONICLE OF THE OLD WEST

Kitchen's hacienda was the model of a feudal estate. There was the sentinel posted on the roof, and all his workers—from the man in the cienaga with the stock to the one plowing in the bottoms—carried rifles. Every man, boy, and women went armed. Revolvers, rifles, and shotguns were located along the walls and in every corner.

The Kitchen family consisted of his wife, Dona Rosa; Crandal, an adopted son; and a great many nieces of his Mexican wife. All together under his care on the ranch he had almost a hundred people. The ranch was more like a village with its own blacksmith, saddler, wagon maker, carpenters, and farm laborers. In addition to his ranch workers, he employed his own soldiers, a band of Opta Indians.

A canny man, Kitchen never traveled the same route twice, and he always slept with one eye open. He was able to resist the Apaches through the constant watchfulness of his employees. In case of an Indian attack, the residents of the complex were experts at a set drill. If attacked, the guard on the roof would discharge his gun as a signal to the workers in the fields. These men would instantly run for the house, while Pete, or his wife, would gather up the guns from the corners and wall racks and lay them out ready for use. She would then tie her skirts around her, making them look like trousers, seize her gun, and help drive the Apaches away.

Only once did things go amiss during an attack. Crandal was with the Mexican laborers in the field and fell asleep in the hay. When a band of Apaches attacked the workers, the Mexicans fled to the house, forgetting about the boy. He woke up just as the Indians were on him. They shot him through the body while he was making the sign of the cross.

When the railroad came to Tucson, the competition of the pork goods it brought adversely affected Kitchen's business. He sold his ranch for a good round figure. Pete Kitchen, the scourge of the Apaches, died peacefully in Old Tucson on August 5, 1895.

CHAPTER 4

The Opportunists

Although the pioneers in the old Southwest experienced many vicissitude, combating Indians and outlaws, besides gambling on the chance of gaining a livelihood on the wild stock ranges and in the mines, they were a resourceful lot and capable of surviving by their wits as well as labor.

—J. S. ALLEN, FEDERAL WRITERS' PROJECT INTERVIEWER

The Arizona Territory offered up miles of gama grazing land that disappeared over a distant horizon. These grasslands were broken by craggy mountains hiding their riches behind stony faces. This land called to cattlemen and shepherds, prospectors and miners, and here many found success. But if it weren't for the opportunist, Arizona would have remained nothing more than grazing land rimmed by beckoning mountain ranges.

The opportunists were the men who entered this world of violence and danger, a place of death and disappointment, and they made it a place of promise and success. A few came with skills such as the lawyers and doctors. However, most brought only their determination and hands that were ready and willing to work. They were the ones who built the infrastructure to supply the ranchers with their needs, and to service the mining camps. Most of them came into this territory without any capital and just had to make good somehow. Some of these hardy and venturesome pioneers seemed to enjoy a so-called "charmed life," but the practical truth of the matter probably is that they were persevering and had "what it takes."

They built villages that grew into towns, then cities. They supplied the daily requirements of food, water, shelter, fuel, and transportation. It was through their determination, their willingness to work hard, and their vision, that the wilderness turned from a land with promise, to a rich territory, and then into a significant state.

The men who first came here needed more than dreams. Preconceived notions of glory and riches were set aside, replaced by meeting challenges with the willingness to do what was needed to persevere in this untamed land. To their advantage, the territory was so raw that there were few rules or expectations on how one was to behave. Unencumbered, these men were able to achieve personal goals, sometimes with violence and sometimes with unscrupulous moves. These personal goals, over time, set the direction for the development of the land, the economy, and the culture of the territory. The goals were not especially altruistic; survival and success were all that mattered. Along the way some became rich, some became famous, and some faded away. However, every one of them marked the road toward statehood and history.

Until 1854 the Southwest was a land defined by myths, adventure stories, and a few official documents. It was also a land coveted by visionaries who had riches on their mind as they dreamed of a rail line joining the East Coast with California. The financial potential was enormous, especially after the discovery of gold at Sutter's Mill in 1848.

An east–west rail line would open trade with Pacific markets, and perhaps give the South much-needed support in their quest for an expanded economy based on slavery and cotton. The northern states saw the rail line as a supply line for resources and manufactured goods.

The Gadsden Purchase of the land below the Gila River from Mexico in 1854 made this vision a reality by supplying the means to develop a southern railroad route. This newly opened western frontier presented an opportunity for men who were willing to take chances and had the courage to meet challenges by making their own rules.

ONE OF THE FIRST

The first white pioneer men to find their way west were the trappers. Among these unorthodox men was Pauline Weaver, who arrived in the

Arizona lands in 1830. Early in life he entered the service of the Hudson Bay Company and stayed with them until, tired of ice and snow, he headed west, following the Green, the Grand, and the Colorado Rivers.

Often he acted as interpreter between the Indians and the white men. The Indians respected his sagacity and his courage and therefore permitted him to come and go unharmed. For some reason he lost the confidence of the Indians, and some young Apache Mohave bucks ravaged his plot of ground while he was off hunting and trapping. He complained to their chief, who laughed. Knowing his reputation was in serious jeopardy, Weaver took his complaint to the commanding office at Fort Whipple and led the soldiers to the camp of the Indians. His intent was to teach the Indians a lesson. Things got completely out of hand, the soldiers attacked, the Indians resisted, and the army destroyed the native band. That was the end of Weaver's prestige. Comprehending his precarious position, he attached himself to Fort Whipple as scout and guide until the day he died.

About midnight the day after the confrontation between Weaver, the army, and the Indians, Weaver, who had been out hunting, was preparing venison and coffee in the fireplace of his cabin when Aha-sa-ya-mo, an Indian maiden, appeared and warned him that her tribesmen were approaching to kill him. He set out for the fort but instead rode straight into an Indian ambush. Although he managed to escape the attack, he suffered wounds from several arrows. One flint arrow remained in his body for the rest of his life, causing him considerable pain.

Not long after this incident, Weaver spotted a soldier trying to run Aha-sa-ya-mo through with his bayonet. Weaver was able to save her, but she, several Indian women, and children were now prisoners jailed at the fort. Weaver told her to have no fear. Four days later when the guardhouse was inspected, the women and children were all missing. The old scout had found a way to help them escape.

Later Weaver worked as a guide and scout at Camp Lincoln. He pitched his tent on the river bottom near a thick shelter of willows apart from the soldiers' quarters. For days at a time he would disappear, hunting or scouting the area. No one thought much of it when they didn't see him for long periods. Weaver was suffering from his wounds. In his painful state he was of little use for scout duty and therefore not much help to the army.

One night the sentinel on duty noticed a light in Weaver's tent far into the night. Late the next afternoon Rice, his fellow scout, went down to visit with Weaver. He noticed single moccasin tracks leading from the willows to the cabin and back again. When Rice approached the tent, he found the door flaps securely tied. Untying them, he opened the tent flaps and went in. Everything was in order. He looked over at the bunk— there lay the old scout, a blanket tucked neatly about his body, a towel laid over his face, and on the table a candlestick containing the drippings of a burned candle.

There was no sign of a struggle or violence. Rice knew then that the Indian girl was true to her friend in death as in life. She was with Weaver at the end.

GOVERNOR SAFFORD'S ARIZONA

There were only two or three American women in Tucson when the newly appointed governor, Anson P. K. Safford, arrived in the summer of 1869. The residents of this small Southwest town were Mexicans and Americans who were, at the time, living in harmony. Life was open and friendly, with many of the social events consisting mainly of balls. If someone wanted to give a ball, he would find a shed, sweep it out, and find a base drum player. Old Joe and his harp would help make music. It wasn't an expensive event. The host had to pay the harpist and provide the candles to light up the shed. The only refreshment served was lemonade ladled out from an olla.

Mothers of the single women attended as *cuidatores* (chaperones). It was a very polite event and everyone was well behaved. If a man got drunk, he could count on his friends putting him where he could safely sleep it off. It was also a romantic time; a fellow in love would show his affection by buying his sweetheart a pair of shoes or by cracking a *caseorons*, eggshells filled with finely cut colored paper, over her hair.

The Shoo Fly restaurant was the chief and most aristocratic eating house in Tucson. It was here that statesmen, including Safford; army officers; gamblers; members of the legal profession; and interesting strangers gathered. The tables were rickety; tablecloths, china, and flatware were crude. The pine benches and leather-bottomed chairs were rough, but there was no lack of good manners and enlightening conversation. The ceiling of this tinted adobe was covered with white muslin. Steady boarders had regular seats and napkins; transients sat where they could and had no cultural device like a napkin.

The name Shoo Fly was indicative of good intentions rather than achieved results, for the place was far from lacking in flies. The earnest and honest landlady hired two soft-voiced Mexican boys and dressed them in white cotton with bright-colored sashes. Their job was to drive the flies away with the fly flappers.

The fare was monotonous, but good. There was meat in abundance, mostly mutton and bacon. Eggs were plentiful and chicken was often served. Potatoes and apples were rare. A pound of apples brought from San Diego by express cost a dollar. When the Apaches allowed, pack trains arrived loaded with oranges, apricots, lemons, and quinces from Hermosillo, Sonora. Honey was a delicacy available sometimes from California, and canned oysters from Guaymas would show upon occasion.

Stewed peaches and prunes were a staple, but now and then half-dried grapes came from the Rio Grande, black figs from Mexico, or, on rare occasions, strawberries. Ice cream showed up for the first time in 1869. It was made by an Italian from Sonora who charged five dollars a quart for what was frozen mush.

Governor Safford appreciated the pleasant social ambiance of the town. His main interest, however, was in the schools of the town. He enjoyed visiting the public school in Tucson once or twice a week. It was on such a visit that he met the boy Bonillas. He learned the poor boy, the son of a blacksmith, stayed out of school a day or two a week working to earn enough money to buy books for his schoolwork. He understood Bonillas's needs. Because of his own childhood poverty, he had no more than a total of five quarters of schooling in his entire life. He was a self-educated man.

Safford told the teacher he would supply the boy with books, paper, and everything necessary so he could attend school regularly. The parents would not let Bonillas their son, accept this offer unless he could do something in return. The governor, aware of pride, employed the school-boy to come in the mornings to sweep his office, black his boots, and feed his mules.

Safford, the third governor of the Arizona Territory, officiated over a land in chaos. There was no telegraph or banks in Safford's Arizona, but there were some safes. Each man took care of his money in his own way. There was ruin everywhere, which was the result of Apache warfare. The settlers charged that General Stoneman and his troops were inactive and useless. The territory lacked a school system. In addition, transportation was difficult and costly, as the nearest railroad was two thousand miles away.

At his own expense, Safford journeyed to Washington, DC, during the first winter after he became governor. He asked the president and Congress for help. Congress provided for the calling of a legislature and gave Governor Safford almost unlimited authority in the interim. General Stoneman was relieved, and Colonel George Crook took over the command in his place.

The governor organized a company of volunteers and led them against the Apaches. Under such fighters as Bob Leatherwood, the motto of the volunteers seemed to be, "First fire; then inquire." Although the settlers fought bravely, the problem was one that only regular soldiers could solve, and eventually they did, thanks to Crook and his methods. Safford continued to clean up the area. He ejected outlaws who came in from Mexico, and he insisted on a proper and consistent enforcement of the laws by the legislature. To pay for his changes, he supported new revenue laws.

Deprived of schooling when he was a child, Safford held a high value for education. The town of Prescott was interested in supporting the education of their children and working with them. In 1873 the governor secured Professor Moses H. Sherman as principal of the Prescott school. Safford probably borrowed the money to pay for Mr. Sherman's traveling expenses from Vermont to Arizona.

The professor organized the school and established a grade system. The new plan grew so rapidly that in 1874 Prescott erected a brick school building and permitted children from all over the area to attend. Other towns followed suit in organizing and supporting the education of their children. Yuma built a schoolhouse; Ehrenburg had plans for a building. Maricopa County raised a subscription to erect a school, and Tucson built a school that could accommodate two hundred pupils.

Safford traveled throughout the territory, visiting settlers to encourage them and to find out their needs. These visits were at his expense and often involved great danger and discomfort. Sometimes he would spend a month or six weeks on one of these tours. Often his friend, gunsmith John S. Vosburg, traveled with him.

Safford seldom swore, but one incident tried even his calm nature. Vosburg and the governor left Wickenburg for Tucson about four o'clock on an early winter day. They expected to travel about thirty miles toward Phoenix and make camp at the cabin of Portuguese Pete. It began to rain, and soon it was so dark they couldn't see where they were. Now and then Vosburg would strike a match to try and find the road. Not having much success with that, they decided to trust the mules.

About eight-thirty that evening they thought they were near Portuguese Pete's, but when they lit a match there was no sign of the cabin. They figured they were off the road and they best make camp where they were.

Safford took the mules and groped around for a place to picket them. He found good grass and tied the mules with forty feet of rope. Vosburg started a fire and collected the cooking utilities. The rain was pouring down, and dinner that night was bacon and hardtack, made soggy by the rain. They unrolled their blankets and made their beds under the buckboard. Sleep was impossible, and the weather got colder and colder as the temperature dropped toward morning.

They kept striking matches and looking at their watches to see the time. At five o'clock, they gave up, as dawn started streaking across the sky.

They hadn't slept more than an hour. The governor collected the mules as Vosburg broke camp and rolled up the soggy blankets.

They traveled about a quarter of a mile, and there was the shack of Portuguese Pete. That's when the governor swore, and did a mighty fine job of it.

Anson Safford served as governor for two terms, a total of eight years. He refused a third term and headed for Florida. He had gained little

Anson Safford, Governor of Arizona and founder of the town of Tarpon Springs, Florida

personal wealth during his governorship, and when he left Arizona, he had the clothes on his back, his mules, and his buckboard. While he was in Florida, the Tombstone mines, one of his business ventures, paid off, although he never made the money that the Scheiffelin Brothers did when they sold their claims. In Florida, he joined with business partners in the purchase of four million acres of land and on a part of that, he developed a town called Tarpon Springs.

ANYTHING TO PERSEVERE

The laissez-faire early environment of the territory suited King S. Woolsey when he set foot on the territory in 1860. A Southerner by birth and training, his early days were hard. He ran away from home and joined a filibustering expedition in Cuba. Captured, he spent several months as a prisoner.

The English Consul in Havana obtained his release and he headed for California, taking work as a miner. Eleven years of digging tugged at him, and he decided to head for Arizona and a more challenging lifestyle. In 1860 he arrived in Yuma. His wealth consisted of a horse, a rifle, and five dollars.

There weren't many jobs available in the tough territory, you took whatever you could find, and Woolsey secured a position as a mule driver. It was one of the lowliest jobs available. He saved enough to buy his own mule team and with it was able to secure a lucrative contract to supply hay for the army. With his government money, he purchase the Agua Caliente Ranch with George Martin as partner.

Cattle rancher Woolsey became a supplier to the California Column during their time in the territory, and this helped make him a wealthy man. By 1863 he earned enough money to venture out in some prospecting speculations in northern Arizona. He discovered gold at Lynx Creek, making enough to buy the Agua Fria Ranch with John Dixon.

Woolsey, like many frontiermen, was always thinking of ways to increase his wealth. Ranchers had difficult cattle trails to travel, and he conceived the idea of building a road into northern Arizona. During the construction, the Indians raided the town of Wickenburg, stealing a considerable amount of cattle. Woolsey formed a posse to chase down the raiders. In the group were several Maricopa Indians who were no friends of the Apaches. The posse caught up with the marauders just beyond the Superstition Mountains, and Woolsey and his posse won the day in a battle that was a bloody massacre.

Woolsey often said, "Driving freight wagons, ranching, mining, keeping stores are business. Fighting Indians and Mexicans is a pleasure." In 1864 he demonstrated his philosophy by leading one hundred men on a twenty-day Indian hunt. In the resulting two fights, Woolsey's party killed thirty-four Indians.

Having succeeded at business, ranching, and prospecting, Woolsey entered politics. He was commissioned a lieutenant colonel in the Arizona Volunteers, appointed by Governor John Goodwin as one of his aids, and was a member of the First Legislature. He also served as a joint councilman from Yavapai and Maricopa Counties. All this was achieved by a former mule driver who was willing to work at anything.

Sam Hughes arrived in the pueblo of Tucson on March 12, 1858, and found a sleepy Mexican village with dirt streets and an abundance of saloons. His first business venture was a trade. He used his good harness to obtain some grain. From grain trading, he went into the butchering business and, according to him, made "money hand over fist."

When the Civil War broke out, Hughes seized the opportunity to increase his business by buying and selling grain, hay, and meat to the overland stage and to supply the stations between Maricopa Wells and Apache Pass. Although he made his money in trade, he saw the advantages of the political life. In 1870, he became the territory's adjutant general, a position he held under two governors. He expanded his political clout by serving as a councilman from 1871 to 1877, and as sheriff of Pima County.

Looking to increase his sphere of influence, and determined to stick his finger in any pie that might yield a profit, Hughes financially backed John Wasson in the establishment of the *Arizona Citizen* newspaper and Sylvester Mowry in the *Arizonan* newspaper.

Hughes spread his money and influence around. He grubstaked a large number of prospectors and lent his support in the development of Tombstone, Harshaw, the Montezuma, and the Washington mining camps. His ventures were eclectic. He organized the first bank in Tucson, and in 1875 opened an assay office near the Pioneer Brewery on North Main Street in Tucson.

He was hardly a modest man, having once said,

> *I helped build churches and schools and spent my time and money on them. My hobby was to make a town. When I was in the legislature, during the administration of Governor Safford, I helped get up good school laws. I offered to help the Mormons build a church, and will yet. I have helped every club and every organization. I helped the different lodges. You see, I owned so much property that I had to do these things to boost my own game. I always encouraged amusements and went in with Tom Fitch in building the first courthouse.*

Hughes's idea of amusements might not be the most acceptable, yet his financial backing, and political wheeling and dealings, were a major influence in creating and establishing Tucson as a major town in the Arizona Territory.

Not all the early settlers became successful politicians and businessmen. Joe Kirby typified the pioneer who eked out a living by supplying the needs of the earlier settlers, and in doing so became one of the first pioneer entrepreneurs. He saw a need and answered it, and in the desert, the biggest need is water.

Kirby sold water to the miners in Helvetia. He charged fifty cents a "burro." A burro was two ten-gallon canvas bags of water. Not all his customers wanted a bag of water. The poorer miners just bought a bucket or two a day. To handle this trade, he attached a cow's horn to the bag opening. He would press the horn up to start the water flowing.

Kirby's best customers were the saloon owners. Perhaps they needed the water to weaken the drinks, as their customers surly didn't go to the saloons to drink water. Usually the saloons bought a load a day, and a load was six burros. They would buy a couple of burro loads of water in the morning, and then again in the afternoon.

Kirby bought his burros in Tucson, paying between two and five dollars each. He obtained the water from a well two and half miles away that he rented from a widow. He paid five cents a bag, ten cents a burro, earning forty-five cents a bag profit. When the widow was away, he paid nothing. He made between twelve to fifteen dollar a day, which was far more than he could make as a miner or ranch hand.

As mines increased, so did the demand for fuel. Kirby saw another possible market and hired a Mexican man to cut mesquite and load it on the burros. He priced this at fifty cents a burro load, one bundle per burro. Unfortunately his latest venture cost him his business; he lost his clients when the mines closed down and the railroad arrived. He went broke in 1894 and took a job as a clerk in one of Tucson's stores.

Levi Jones arrived in Prescott in 1880, the same year the railroad entered Tucson. Jones was typical of the men arriving in those days. He was resourceful, capable of surviving by his wits as well as his labor. He arrived without capital and with a determination to make good somehow. Jones worked as a freighter, cowboy, and livestock trader and was either flushed with money or hard up, although he took advantage of every opportunity that presented itself.

Visiting with some freighters at the City Corral saloon in Prescott, he learned of the predicament of a contractor who had taken the job to move a great granite boulder into town from the hills about three miles away. It was a good joke, as the contractor was doomed to fail. The huge rock was the base for the bronze equestrian statue of Bucky O'Neil, to be erected in the Plaza. The contractor was to receive one thousand dollars for moving the boulder, but the job was too much for his outfit.

Curious, Levi Jones got on his horse and rode out to inspect this problematic boulder. After viewing the huge rock, he galloped back to town to see the authorities and offered to do the job. Within the hour, Jones rounded up a bunch of freight horses, gathered chains and other

Tucson 1800
AUTHOR'S COLLECTION

tools, and was on his way out to the rock. He cut down trees, rigged up a pole sled, and at three o'clock that afternoon, amidst a great cloud of dust and hell-bent shouting, Jones triumphantly signaled the big team to stop, with the boulder resting on the exact agreed upon spot. He made over eight hundred dollars profit—not bad for a man who lived by his wits.

THE FREIGHTERS

The Gadsden Purchase in 1854 gave the United States the land for a southern railroad route that would join the East and West Coasts. However, it also created a problem with the indigenous Native American tribes who did not take kindly to possession of their lands and the elimination of their hunting grounds. They retaliated by attacking the railroad workers, the construction sites, and the small villages cropping up along the railroad lines. Whether it was never considered, or the government underestimated its significance, the indigenous Indian population became a big problem. To protect its business interest in the West, and its people, the government constructed over fourteen army camps and forts.

During the late 1860s and early 1870s, after the Civil War, the US Army committed eight thousand of their eleven thousand personnel to protecting their western lands.

Along with the army posts and the arrival of the railroad builders in the Southwest came the demand for goods. Delivering these essential items provided a highly profitable business for freighters, who were some of the earliest businessmen of the West.

The profit was enormous for the early freighters, and many of them put their money in other businesses such as commercial buildings, ranches, politics, or resorts. This group of futuristic-thinking men was willing to take a chance on some far-reaching projects, and in the end they tamed the wilderness of the West into settled communities, towns, and cities.

The early long-distance freight teams usually consisted of twelve mule teams. Caravans of these teams owned by primary Arizona firms like Tully and Ochoa, the Samaniegos, and Aquirres, worked their trade from Tucson north to army posts, and to towns such as Phoenix, Prescott, Yuma, and the mining camps.

Freighting was a dangerous occupation in the early West. Joe Winsor remembers passing by Cedar Spring Hills, where nearly all of Samaniego's teamsters died in an attack by Cochise's Apache Indians. Winsor saw the burned-out wagons and fresh graves. Freighters needed to be on constant alert for possible Indian attacks.

The poor road were another challenge. They called the road from the railroad depot in Tucson to Globe the "Great Highway of Danger," because it combined both Indian problems and hard trails. After leaving the hill towns, the road led through the length of the Apache Indian Reservation. Here the teams always traveled in military order. The larger outfits had strict rules of defense. Each night the wagons formed a circle for protection, placing the horses in the middle for safety. Each driver had a pistol and rifle, and each swamper was similarly armed. A swamper was the general flunky around the camps who also served as a night herder.

Sometimes a freighter, eager to earn extra pay or seeking a quick trip, drove ahead of the cloud of dust that always enveloped each large convoy and pushed on alone. Frequently, the next day, the convoy passed the destroyed wagons of these impatient freighters. Nearby would be the bodies of the tortured and murdered teamsters.

The wiser and more careful freighters waited at the railroad depot until a score of wagons were gathered. Then this convoy would proceed northward in relative security because of their united vigilance. The freighters gained some additional safety when, after diplomatic negotiations, the railroad agent paid the Apaches eight hundred thousand dollars in silver coins for the right of way through the reservation.

Freighters did more than deliver the goods. They were responsible for establishing some of Arizona's earliest roads and towns. Freighting originally followed trails made by Indians or wildlife. With repeated use, heavier loads, and the ravages of nature, many of these trails deteriorated to the point where they were unusable, forcing freighters to create new trails.

Al West and his father were contract haulers in 1896 working mostly around the Globe countryside. One of their routes, from Globe to Midland City and Central Heights, ran up the canyon to Burch and back toward what is now the Globe-Miami Country Club and golf course. This covered a distance of nine miles, three as the crow flies, but the mountains prevented this direct route, and all agreed that a route directly over the mountains was impassable on foot or horseback or by any sort of vehicle.

Saloons can be creative places, and one night West and his friends were sharing drinks and ideas at a bar in Globe. The subject came up about an old trail, and after much discussion, the men agreed that a road should be made of this trail. Such a road would cut off six or seven miles of travel between Globe and Russell Gulch.

Filled with bravado and booze, West declared he could drive a team and a wagon over the mountain trail, and would do it if any of the men would go with him. His pals agreed to help him try, if he would wait until the next day. "No, we won't wait until tomorrow. We will go tonight," demanded West.

The party left the barroom and found a big team of mules hitched to a heavy wagon. It was the property of the Inspiration Mine. They appropriated the rig and set out across the mountains. It was a wild ride made more so by the night. At one place, they had to go over a barbed-wire fence. They didn't have pliers to cut the wire, so they pulled up several sections and laid the posts and wires down on the ground. A few men stood on the barbed wire fencing, keeping it close to the ground, while the team drove over it. Once the outfit was over the fence, they put it back up again and headed for the cabin of the fence owner to report what they had done to his property.

Fully expecting to get a good dressing down, they were surprised when the owner only asked them which way they had come. The route sounded good to the owner, and he began to use the trail regularly for hauling loads to Globe. It wasn't long before the trail was improved, traffic increased, and it became the first road from Globe to Central Heights, Inspiration Mine, and the Miami district.

In 1897 Joe Winsor was hauling merchandise for the Alexander Brothers. One particular freight load was for Mr. Boardman, a storekeeper in Payson. This was a trial run to see if it was cheaper to haul from Geronimo or Flagstaff.

They loaded up at Geronimo in August and took a route through Globe and the wheat fields. They crossed the Salt River, where Roosevelt Lake is now, went up the Tonto, across the Rye, and up Rye Creek. When they reached the Ox Bow Mountain, they first tried pulling their trail wagons with six mules each. It didn't work, and they finally had to use twelve mules per wagon to get up Ox Bow.

It turned out to be a fine trip. The grass was good, and Winsor turned his animals out to graze. The hard work made them both thirsty and hungry. The cook had plenty of food, and there were two barrels of whiskey and two barrels of wine. Joe Elmer was the cook and bartender, and Winsor was the horse manager. The selection of libations was generous. Elmer would ask the teamsters if they wanted lemonade, sour wine, or sour whiskey with their meal. They carried a load of lemons and oranges, which they used to flavor their drinks.

Although it took twenty days to complete this trip, they were well fortified. They supplemented their food supply with the flocks of quail they saw along the route. However, the trip was not without problems. Driving along Dry Creek the teamsters found much of the road washed out and had to create their own road as they traveled this route.

Winsor, as a driver for his father's freighting company, never knew what kind of problems he would face. On one of their trips from Wilcox to Globe, he came to a dry wash. He had a twelve-mule team with three wagons hooked on, and the sandy wash was too much for the heavy wagons. To get the stuck team going, he shoveled the sand out from in front of the wheels.

While shoveling, about eight little Indian boys came up beside the road to watch. When he was done shoveling, he got back in the wagon and hollered, "Get up!" One of the Indian boys hollered, "Whoa!" That immediately stopped the mules before they were out of the wash, and the wagons sunk back down into the sand. Winsor got down, walked forward, and started shoveling again.

This occurred three or four times. Winsor would shovel, get back on the wagon, and yell at the mules, and the little boy would holler, "Whoa!" Each time the mules halted, and each time the wagons settled back into the sand. Winsor's temper was rising. Again he shoveled dirt, and this time, when finished, he gave the mules a little tap with the shovel to get them all lined up. When he was opposite the Indian boy, he hit him over the head with the shovel. You could hear the kid bawl for a mile.

Since they were near the Indian teepees, it was only a few minutes before the Indian squaws were all there. Meanwhile Winsor's father had traveled a half a mile on and pulled up, then came back to help just as his son hit the Indian boy. The elder Winsor admonished his sixteen-year-old son: "Why Joe, you will have every damned Indian on the reservation here before we know it. They will be after us." With that, he took down a sack of sugar and gave a few dimes and quarters to the boy's mother. He always brought a hundred-pound sack of sugar along on trips as peace offerings, and he seldom had any sugar left after making a trip across the reservation.

While a certain resource could lead to a new freighting contract, it could also lead to an unpredictable result. Isaac Solomon never thought that in 1872, by accepting a contract to supply desert ironwood to the ore furnaces in Clifton, he would found not one, but two towns.

The area from which he operated offered what seemed to be an inexhaustible supply of wood in the dense forests between Safford and the town of Duncan. Charles Overlock, who built the first residence there, developed the water supply, and was the town's first mayor, founded this town.

Solomon hired three hundred Mexicans to cut the wood and handle the burro pack trains for him. The working Mexicans formed a small village and called it San Jose. Meanwhile, one mile away, Solomon founded the town of Solomonville.

Freighting led to other occupations and business ventures for the early haulers. Some had no choice, circumstances forced them out of freighting, and others, viewing the railroad as a major threat, looked to invest in such things as land, businesses, and politics.

Oscar Buckalew started as a freighter with the firm of Tully and Ochoa in 1863, carrying express mail from Tubac to the Patagonia Mine. In 1867 the Apaches attacked the mine and Buckalew rode in to aid the miners. Around the mouth of the mine was an adobe corral that enclosed the mine building. Tom Yerkes, Tom Gardner, Richard Dorce, and E. N. Marcy holed up in the corral to take a stand against the attack. Buckalew was galloping toward the corral gate when a bullet hid his leg and downed his horse. The fall pinned him under the horse, smashing the leg. Tom Yerkes and Tom Gardner rushed out to rescue the downed man and managed to bring him inside the corral. After the attack, they sent him to Tubac, where doctors amputated his leg above the knee.

With driving no longer an option, Buckalew turned to other sources for earning a living. He found a place in the early political environment of Pima County serving as a clerk for the First Judicial District Court, then in 1870 as county recorder. He was the county treasurer in 1872 and a member of the Third Territorial Legislature. In 1870 he formed a partnership with Joe Ochoa in a new freighting business. In 1873 he built a block of adobe structures on Alameda Street in Tucson, just north of the city plaza, which cost him twenty thousand dollars, and by 1881 he gave his occupation as "Capitalist." He added to his wealth in 1885 by securing the profitable contract of transporting the Sixth Regiment of the US cavalry from Santa Fe to Arizona.

For twelve years, John J. Gardiner hauled supplies from Yuma to Tucson, Camp Grant, Prescott, and various mining camps along the way, with his five wagons outfitted with ten mules each. His loads often weighed as much as six tons.

An innovative thinker, and an ambitious man, he left the freighting business in 1886 and invested in Phoenix property, building one of the first hotels, a one-story adobe building with a swimming pool. Gardiner had a small channel dug from the acequia, an irrigation ditch, along the west side of Third Street. The channel flowed into a deep excavation in the inside court of the hotel. The overflow water from this "pool" flowed into another small ditch along the north side of Washington Street. A canvas house covered the pool.

Former freighter Leopoldo Carrillo added one of the most pleasing venues to the town of Tucson. Earning his money freighting between Yuma, Tucson, and El Paso, he turned his attention to the addition of a pleasure resort for the growing town.

The Carrillo Gardens was a landscaped wooded park and pleasure site that included a small lake for boating, a saloon, a bathhouse, and refreshment stands. Carrillo brought vines and trees from California and Mexico and had them planted in artistic arrays. The gardens featured a small zoo, with races by monkeys on ponies. Dancing and shooting galleries added to the entertainment offerings for young and old.

In 1875, when Carrillo went to Sonora, Mexico, for business, he was captured during a fight between the state troops and the rebels. They held him prisoner until his wife paid the fifteen-thousand-dollar ransom.

Some businesses were more prolific than other endeavors. In 1872, Phoenix had fifteen saloons. Eight dealt exclusively in liquors, a few more sold other merchandise with their whiskey stock. Duncan had seven saloons and two grocery stores. A rough town, Duncan decorated the outside of their saloons by sticking green cottonwood posts to be use as hitching posts. Since the town had no jail, the posts were also used to chain prisoners until it was decided they were safe enough to turn loose.

FRONTIER PROFESSIONALS

The frontier West was not exactly the place a new physician or lawyer could count on making his fortune, but that didn't stop men who had adventuresome blood cursing through their veins.

In 1874, when W. A. Wood completed his medical training in his home state of Missouri, he decided to take his medical knowledge where he thought there was the greatest need, and the fewest doctors. He headed west in a covered wagon and reached Tucson in May of that year.

His first job was as the physician with the Green Cattle Company for their cowboys and their families. His pay was room and board. He spent two years with the Green Cattle Company and, realizing the skills needed for a frontier doctors, he returned to St. Louis for surgical study. Two years later, he returned to Tucson, bringing his new knowledge and a load of medical supplies.

Early Tucson had no hospitals and very little in the way of medical supplies. Wood ordered what he needed from St. Louis and had his supplies shipped by freight cars to the end of the line. From there the supplies continued on by whatever transportation was available. Arrival dates were unpredictable, as was the condition of the goods when received. It wasn't until 1880 that the railroad finally reached Tucson, providing the most dependable transportation for men and goods.

The search for attacking Indian bands was part of frontier life. Pioneers lived with the knowledge that no matter where they were, or what they were doing, they would be fighting the Apaches, and that these fights would take a certain toll of lives.

Wood traveled from St. John to Tucson administering medical care. When he traveled alone, which he did frequently, the Indians never bothered him. When he was with a group of men or an army troop, he would help fight off the frequent Apache attacks.

When the Indians made a raid on a small settlement below St. John and carried off some cattle and supplies killing several people, Wood joined the hunt. The next morning with fifty other men, the doctor followed the savages, but they were unable to overtake the raiders until near nightfall. The pose reached a spring with a partially constructed shack covered with poles. They decided to stop there and water their horses.

Suddenly a shot zinged above the heads of the men who were at the spring. The attack came from the top of the mountain. Cover was not good at the spring or the shack, and by the time darkness fell, causalities included two dead men and one wounded man. The men fired at the spurts of light from the guns of the Indians, but because of the darkness they had no way of knowing how effective their shots were.

With darkness, the attack ceased. Believing they would be safer if they were at another spot by daylight, the men tried to retrace their steps. They knew troops from Fort Thomas were somewhere in the vicinity, and they set out hoping to reach them. They traveled an hour, thinking they were on their way to safety, when the Indians attacked from in front of them. The band had managed to get ahead of them and set up an ambush.

Expecting a full-scale charge, the men were surprised that the Indians withdrew after firing only a few shots. The men found the troops the next day, and the whole group, soldiers and frontiersmen, set out on the trail of the attackers.

Dr. Wood was used to administering to wounded pioneers. He never denied anyone care, nor did he ask too many questions. One afternoon a man rode into the doctor's camp on the Gila River and fell off his horse and onto the doctor's doorstep. He had a bullet in his arm. The stranger was weak and pale from the loss of blood. Wood extracted the bullet and treated the wound. The man stayed with the doctor for some time while he recovered. However, he was always on guard, constantly keeping a wary eye out for pursuers.

Wood knew the man must be a fugitive from justice or his own outlaw band, but invoking the code of the West, the doctor never questioned the patient. In time the wounded man felt he needed to move on. He pressed a large sum of money on Dr. Wood, far more than he would have received for his services. The good doctor never did know whom he healed.

Pioneers were not Wood's only patients. He worked with the Indians as well. Indian men seldom came for treatment, nor would they cooperate with the doctor. But the women had more confidence in Wood's medical skills and frequently would bravely seek him out.

One night an Indian man came into the doctor's camp and insisted he follow him to his teepee on the reservation. The doctor went with him and upon arriving found his wife about to deliver a child. She would not permit an examination. All he could do was watch and wait. It wasn't long before she gave birth to a fine big boy. Dr. Wood saw there was another baby on its way. He told the woman, "Another," and held up two fingers.

"No," she emphatically said.

Wood explained to the husband that another baby would arrive in fifteen or twenty minutes. "No," he answered, and nothing the doctor could say would convince any of the Indians present that another birth was about to take place. The husband said women gave birth to one child at a time. He knew his tribe's history and was adamant on this point. When the second baby arrived, the Indians looked upon the doctor with awe, some thought he was superhuman, others believed he was responsible for the event.

Dr. Wood was not the only medical man in the territory in 1872. Dr. Thibode was in Wickenburg, and Dr. Forbes practiced in Tucson. A wit of the times wrote, "In case the Apaches kill their victims outright the doctors will have to follow the honorable profession of adobe making for a living."

TAMING THE WILD WEST

Danger came in many forms in the Old West. Living in towns provided a degree of security, but brought with it a trade-off for other dangers. Fires were always a potential factor in the wooden towns of the Old West. J. Ivancovich lost his Tucson fruit store when a fire started about midnight. When the alarm sounded, the town men rush to douse the fire with their collapsible leather buckets. They placed a ladder on the building wall, filled the buckets, and passed them up to the men situated along the ladder at various places. These men heaved the water on what burning parts they could reach.

Frontier life was unpredictable, but that didn't necessarily mean pioneers had to do away with some of the comforts and small pleasures of everyday life. If there is a need, and the potential of a profit, someone would find a way to supply the requirement. From butcher to baker to barber, men answered the call, and in looking after their own necessities of life, they helped to civilize the towns and villages. They added their unique brand of business to the frontier, sometimes causing unusual problems.

J. Bauerlein was the first baker in the frontier village of Phoenix. He used a small furnace made of adobe. As simple as his business was, he had his problems. The local newspaper reported in 1872 that, "last Tuesday the town had no bread, and the baker had a holiday because an innocent dog upset the yeast." Bauerlein solved his early problems and was so successful that by August 9 of that year he had to "pull down his oven and build a new one."

The first Chinese arrived in Phoenix in June 1872. The three males and two females started a much-needed laundry. That same year Pete Holcomb partnered with E. T. Hargraves to open a meat market. Holcomb killed the steer, cut it in quarters, and hung it up. Hargraves took care of the commercial end of the business. All customers cut off what they wanted, furnished their own knives, and paid from twenty-five to thirty cents a pound, depending on the cut.

After working for nine years as a miner, Ed Wittig decided there was an easier way to make a living. He went to work as an apprentice barber and opened his own shop in Tombstone. The cowboys and miners cleaned up and got their hair cut only once every four or five months. There wasn't much profit from them. However, since they wore the hair long, he made nearly as much money trimming hair as cutting it. Twenty-five cents was the price of a haircut, fifteen cents for a shave. He did a lot of singeing the tips of hair, as it was supposed to preserve the hair oils and give a smooth look.

Merchants arrived in small towns and opened up stores that catered to the needs of frontier families. The Allisons never planned on going into the mercantile business, but life on the frontier demanded flexibility. They kept their options open and tried just about everything. They arrived in Tucson in 1875 and started out farming. Eventually they opened a store in the Washington Mine camp. When that closed, they opened a butcher shop in Harshaw. In 1881, the family became part of the Tucson commercial community when they established a store on Convent Street.

In the late 1880s, Christopher Layton also joined the primary merchants of the territory when he established the first creamery and ice plant in Graham County.

Other pioneers making their mark in the commercial side of frontier life included the Goldwater brothers. Joe and Mike Goldwater opened a store in Phoenix. They started their enterprise by purchasing a large stock of goods and offering ready-made items and raw materials to frontier families.

Merchandising came with its own dangers. Businesses did not always run smoothly. In addition to financial worries, there were dangers brought on by the rough frontier life. The Goldwaters ran into this trouble when they were driving along the road from Prescott to Ehrenberg on store business. According to the Arizona *Sentinel* of June 22, 1872, the Goldwaters and Dr. W. W. Jones were traveling in two buggies. Fourteen miles later, near Mint Valley, they were attacked by Apaches. According to the newspaper, "The three gentlemen could, of course, offer no resistance, and their only means of escape was to outrun the Indians. The band pursued them for about four miles down the road, when they fortunately met a party of white men traveling in the direction of Prescott. This additional strength caused the savages to abandon the fracas and head out to their mountain hideaways for safety."

During this cowardly Indian attack, Joe Goldwater received a shot in the back, somewhere over the shoulder blade. His brother Mike had two balls through the rim of his hat, and Dr. Jones escaped with only a few bullet holes through his shirt and coat. They drove to Skull Valley, about eighteen miles from the point of attack. Once there, Dr. Jones was able to examine the wound received by Mr. Goldwater. He probed it but never was able to find the ball.

As towns grew, so did the need to get the news out, especially in booming mining areas such as Tombstone. John Clum arrived in Arizona in 1880. Before he left his home, he sent a small press, some type, and other materials necessary for printing a newspaper out west by covered wagon. That was the beginning of the Tombstone *Epitaph*, one of the frontier West's most famous papers. Clum was also the mayor of Tombstone at the time of the Earp–Clanton feud. He instructed his marshal, Wyatt Earp, to fire first in any clash with outlaws because "an officer of the law is too valuable to take chances with lawbreakers and rustlers."

When Charles Overton arrived in the territory, he too recognized the need and the demand for news. With his help, the Bisbee *Review* was born in 1896.

Delivering the Message

Some news was so urgent, and so current, it couldn't wait for newspaper or handbill announcements. Some news was really history in the making, and John Addison Hunt had no idea he was going to be part of history when he woke up that morning.

He was only seventeen at the time and one of the four drivers who carried mail from Holbrook to Fort Apache. Getting ready for his run one morning, a messenger told him Lieutenant George W. Gatewood wanted to see him at the Holbrook Hotel. That worried Hunt; he feared the lieutenant had heard he was a bit young to be carrying the US mail.

Full of apprehension, he hitched up the team, drove over to the hotel, and tied the mules to the hitching post. He found Lieutenant Gatewood in the lobby, sitting at the writing desk, his back to the doorway. Not wanting to disturb the officer too suddenly, Hunt cleared his throat to draw the man's attention, then announced, "I'm the driver." The army officer rose to his feet, turned quickly around, sized up the driver, then said, "Son, you're too young to be a US mail carrier."

Hunt explained that his brother was holding the job, but he was taking a vacation and with the consent of the contractor, he was filling his place. With that explanation, Gatewood picked up a large envelope lying on the desk and stepped over to the young mail carrier and said,

> Son, I have a message here that is the most important that you will ever have the honor to carry. It goes to General Nelson A. Miles, telling him of the capture of the old outlaw Apache Chief Geronimo. I don't know where you will find the General, but he is in the vicinity somewhere. I just came back from down in Old Mexico where the outlaw band recently surrendered. This message must be delivered at all hazards. Now, are you the man to deliver this message?

Hunt put the message in his inside coat pocket and left Holbrook with the mail.

The mail drivers were warned by the contractors to take no chances in high water with the US mail. However, on reaching the Rio Puerco, three miles out of Holbrook, Hunt found a raging torrent. He had crossed the night before, and it was at its highest safe limits, but this morning it had risen a foot and a half. The flood also covered an area that was now more than three hundred yards wide.

Hunt was faced with a dilemma, He knew it was dangerous to drive into that river with the mail, he also realized the message from Lieutenant Gatewood had to be delivered at "all hazards." It was a difficult decision. If he went back to Holbrook and told the officer he was afraid to cross the river, Gatewood would probably think he should never have entrusted the message to a kid.

There were three mailbags to be delivered that morning. Each one was about half full, and the buckboard was very light. Fortunately, Hunt had drawn the best team in the system from the sixteen teams of horses who were in motion at all times. Not willing to seem incompetent, Hunt decided to take care of the job. He took the first mailbag, put it on the spring seat, doubled it half over, mashed it down flat, took the second mailbag, put it on the first, doubled that over, and sat on it, mashing it flat. He put the third mailbag on the other two, also doubling it over. When he had all the mail on the spring seat, he sat on it, putting his feet out on the dashboard. With this arrangement, he figured he could let four feet of water pass over the buckboard without getting wet or injuring the mail encased in the solid leather bags.

Hunt slipped Gatewood's message into his inside pocket. He buttoned his coat from top to bottom so the message could not slip away from him in case something happened while crossing the raging water. Hunt figured it was a matter of life or death, and he wasn't sure he would be able to stem that river's force. He would rather drown trying to deliver the message than go back and tell the officer he was afraid to cross the swollen stream.

The horses walked into the water up to their sides. The driver saw the rushing current swirling in front of the buckboard. When the horses pitched off into the current, he snapped them with his whip so they would lunge through the current before it had time to turn the buckboard over. When he got through one current, the horses would again walk through deep water, and then would lunge when they crossed the current. There were at least a half a dozen deep current pockets, and the whole river was one of the biggest in Arizona. Although the water ran across the buckboard, the only real danger was when they hit a hole that was deeper than usual.

The next town was twelve miles away. When Hunt arrived in Woodruff, he changed teams and started for Snowflake. He thought he would find General Miles in Fort Apache, a hundred miles away. Fifteen miles east of Snowflake, he saw the big government ambulance coming down the road. It was drawn by some flashy fast-stepping government mules. Hunt knew the driver of that ambulance was one of the crankiest men around. He would only take orders from government officers, and he even hated to do that. Hunt was aware that he had to stop that ambulance because the general might be in it, so he commenced to figure out how he was going to get the driver to stop.

He drove his team to one side and tied it to a cedar tree. He stood in the middle of the road and waved that large envelope Gatewood had given him back and forth for the driver to see. The closer the ambulance got to Hunt, the faster it came. Hunt stood his ground in the middle of the road, and it looked like the driver was going to drive right over him. When the wagon was almost on top of him, the driver yelled and put on the brake. Everything stopped with a jar.

Hunt stepped up close to the driver and asked, "I have a message for General Miles. Is he on this ambulance?" The old general, who was sitting inside, heard Hunt and pushed the door open. "Right this way, son, I'm the man." Hunt stepped up and handed the envelope to the general, who tore it open and read the contents immediately. He read it through a second time before he said anything, then he turned to the young mail carrier and spoke, "Son, that is the most important message it will ever be your privilege to carry." The general said the government of the United States had been trying for years to capture the old outlaw Apache chief and now they had. The seventeen-year-old stood there, with his hand slipped under his arm, and told the general he was proud to have the privilege of carrying a message like that.

Later Hunt learned that while Geronimo and the members of his band were in camp in the mountains of Old Mexico, Lieutenant Gatewood left his detachment and went alone to see Geronimo. The army man told the chief that he was playing a losing game in fighting against the US Army. They would get him sooner or later, and if he persisted, the army would not show him or his people any mercy, they would all be exterminated. However, if he surrendered peaceably, the government would grant him all the mercy possible.

General Nelson A. Miles who waged war against the Apaches

Geronimo surrendered. He, and his faithful tribesman Patches, were taken to Bowie, Arizona and from there to Louisiana. Later the government deported the families and other members of Geronimo's band to Florida.

SHOWTIME

There wasn't much Tom Wills wouldn't do to earn an honest dollar, so when he met Charlie Meadows, better known as "Arizona Charlie," and it was suggested they put together a Wild West show, Wills was anxious to hear the details. A former star attraction with the Buffalo Bill Cody Wild West Show, Arizona Charlie was famous for presenting a rip-roaring show of his own when he could find the finances.

When Wills and Meadows met a certain young man who they took to calling "the Kid" (who also had a large sum of money), they got him so excited about the show he was almost begging to invest. Wills and Arizona Charlie immediately set about organizing the troupe. They bought a big car and a team of the biggest horses they could find. They renovated the car and put in bunks. They purchased tents and camping equipment and spent a lot of time making and gathering scenes for the acts. Wills went to a Maricopa Indian village and hired sixteen braves, including their chief, picking the ones with long hair and the fiercest looks. Next they bought a Concord stage and practiced the act.

The cast had five cowboys and a stage driver. Wills was chief of the cowboys and played many roles in the show. The cowboys did rodeo work, such as roping and tying down steers, riding bucking horses, and other stunts. The show advertised that Wills would ride anyone's bucking horse, or any wild bucking horse, no matter how savage. The show backed this up with the offer of two hundred dollars to the owner if the horse threw him. Arizona Charlie was the master of ceremonies and the barker. He did feat exhibits such as shooting down eggs, riding bucking horses, and performing stunts on running horses.

The trapper cabin and Indian attack scenes never missed stirring the audience into a pitch of excitement. In the act, a trapper and his pretty daughter lived alone in the woods. The Indians would creep down to the cabin and suddenly attack. They grabbed firebrands and burned the trapper and his daughter out of the cabin. Grabbing the trapper, the Indians tied him to a stake, set it afire, and danced around the burning pyre.

Sometimes, for a change of scenario, the trapper died in the fight and the girl was the one tied to the stake. Other times Prince Charming didn't come to her rescue and she would burn. Wills and Arizona Charlie had several variations and played night after night to a packed house. The audience never knew what they were going to see.

Usually before the fair maiden burned, or if her father was burning and she was a prisoner, Wills came galloping in with his cowboys, and with a whoop and a yell he rescued the young woman. The cowboys fought the Indians, firing blanks, and no fire-eaters ever fought harder.

Of course the cowboys drove the Indians away and in the fight killed some. In the end, the girl fell in a faint in the arms of the chief cowboy. It was great fun. The truth, however, was that if Wills was in a real Indian fight he probably would have run as fast as he could in the other direction. Bravery is easy when it's show business.

In another act, the Concord stage came driving around the front of the show among the crowd, and the barker announced that the stage was about to start. This was to get the crowd involved. People paid their fare and climbed in the coach. Wills rode in the front. He was the armed escort.

As they rode around, a band of masked men armed with six shooters came at them and held up the stage. This usually caused the women to scream, as they thought it was a real holdup. The act went over big. There was shooting, and although blanks, they made a great deal of noise.

On May 3, 1883, Arizona Charlie's Wild West Show left Phoenix headed for San Bernardino, California. Wills lived in Bakersfield as a boy, and the Kid grew up in Santa Barbara. They both knew Southern California, and they were convinced they would show up the townsfolk. They practiced and limbered up and then put on a grand opening. They distributed handbills, and posters announced, *Arizona Charlie's Wild West Show, the greatest Wild West Show on earth* was opening in San Bernardino. The people crowded the streets to see the show parade and packed the show. Flush with their success in San Bernardino, the show headed for Los Angeles, then continued on to Bakersfield, Tulras, Visalia, Hanford, and Stockton. It was in Stockton that Wills was injured.

They camped in a grassy field with good water in Stockton. Wills was roping the steers when his horse stepped into an unseen hole hidden by the high grass. He catapulted over his horse and turned a somersault. As he landed, his horse fell over him, hitting him between the legs. They carried him out to a hotel, where he stayed for nine days. The crew continued on to San Francisco and was able to put on a successful show without one of their stars.

Wills could not join the show until his leg healed. He hired Bob Lee to take his place while he recovered, but the cast and Bob did not get along. Quarrels broke out among them. In Oakland someone used a real bullet and nearly hit Bob. That gave the show a bad name and people, ever cautious, stayed away, and the outfit went broke. The Kid lost twenty-five or thirty thousand dollars.

Charlie Meadows quit in high dudgeon and disgust. The strife in the tent took away everyone's enthusiasm and the fun out of doing the show. The Wild West show broke up; the sheriff seized it and sold it at auction. Wills headed back to the range where he belonged.

WALKING SMITH

He said his name was Smith, ". . . just one of the Smith boys, born, let's say, John Smith." It was an ordinary name, a common name, but the man who bore it was far from common. He was an exceptional musician who brought the pleasure of his talent to everyone he met, and he met an extraordinary amount of people across the territory. He reached them not with some flashy or fast-moving vehicle, but by walking.

At eight, Smith was an orphan living with his uncle in Louisiana. He wasn't quite twelve when he walked away from the slavery, both his and that of the blacks, on his uncle's plantation. No one thought enough to look for him; to the world he was just one of the Smith boys, on his own, turned loose in the world.

While working in his uncle's fields he learned from the slaves to pick the banjo, play the French harp and the Jews harp, play the mandolin, and beat the sticks in accompaniment to other instruments. According to Smith, music had possessed his soul.

Even at his young age, he was handy with a six-gun and hot tempered. Consequently it wasn't long before he was in trouble. That's when he met Peter Smith. Although they shared the same last name, they were no relation. That didn't stop Peter Smith from becoming the most important person in John Smith's life. Peter Smith was a tutor of music. The young boy called him the "Maestro," and considered him one of the greatest musicians of the time. For a vagabond, Peter Smith was surprising well versed in books and languages.

The Maestro taught the young boy music, along with the essential things of life. He led the way, and the boy followed willingly, worshipping every move. Together they led the lives of traveling musicians. Eventually the boy helped the Maestro with his music classes as they traveled from one community to another.

They always walked; the elder Smith spurned any other means of travel. "We are the walking musicians, my lad," he would say. "We come closer to the hearts of the people this way." They earned their way giving lessons, entertaining, or when times were lean, playing cards. Peter Smith was a gambling wizard and taught his prodigy some gaming tricks. The two would land in a community dusty, dirty, and travel worn. In spite of their condition, they were always welcomed. When they departed, they left the people with something they could never forget . . . the gift of music.

In 1880, John Smith lost the Maestro to a gunshot wound. He buried him on the Mescalero Indian Reservation in New Mexico. He buried him like an Indian, with all his earthly possessions, except for his violin, a Stradivarius that his companion willed to him. Years later someone stole the valuable instrument, and Smith never recovered it.

After the Maestro died, John Smith continued traveling alone. With his violin he spread music around. He hid his grief at the loss of his friend with his playing. For over fifty years, he shared the joy, grief, and tragedies of remote communities. He traveled every state in the Union, some several times. Occasionally he ran into a relative, or heard about one, but to him they were merely Smiths.

He suffered the thirst and heat of the desert, and the cold and hunger of the mountains. He lived with wild tribes including the Apaches, Navajos, and the Yaquis and never feared for his life. He sat in Indian counsel circles, smoked peace pipes, and ate the flesh of the dog and the rattler with the Indians who wore fresh, white scalps dangling from their belts. His first trip through the Arizona Territory was in 1869. In his Arizona travels, he met Geronimo, Nana, and Cochise and called them all friends.

In his wanderings, Walking Smith met righteous citizens, and outlaws. He treated them the same. He taught the Apache Kid to play the harmonica. The Kid had music in his soul and would have been a great musician but for his background. Smith blamed the Kid's outlaw ways to his outcast status as a half-breed.

Smith also knew Billy the Kid. He gave him lessons on the guitar and played at many social gatherings with him. The musician had some philosophical thoughts on his friend Billy:

If he wants to be dead, and there is a grave over at old Fort Sumner to prove it, whose business is it whether it is true or not? Did anybody ever dig into that grave for proof? Chances are there is a body there all right. What is the difference whose body it may be? If he or any other man can escape death or punishment by the law for crimes that were committed under such circumstance as were his, by going down through the grave, isn't that enough?

If he is alive today, he would be a lonely old man living because life refused to leave his body. He would be an old man laughing up his sleeve at the stupidity of modern laws and the curiosity that killed the cat, and he would be muttering, "Now don't they wish they knew!"

Pat Garret was also a friend of John Smith's. "Pat was a man after my own heart. His record . . . clean, fearless, upstanding . . . did not flatter him. He was even more than that. He was a friend to me."

Smith's musical life was at times dangerous. Often in his youth he fiddled his way out of a tight spot. In the early 1890s he was in an outlaw camp in the Chihuahua Mountains. The boss of that camp was Lee Wright, known then as Lee Woods. Lee liked to beat up his young wife, especially when he was drinking. Lee began arguing with his wife Ellen over the absence of salt in the shaker. Then he slapped her halfway across the cabin.

When Smith objected to the rough treatment of the woman, the outlaw leader backed him against the wall and put the muzzle of cold steel in his belly. He stared at Smith with sinister, terrorizing eyes. His voice sounding like the knell of doom, demanded, "Start playing that damned fiddle." Someone shoved the fiddle into Smith's hands, and the notes of "Buffalo Gals" filled the room.

"Hell play a 'Soldier's Joy,'" ordered Wright, "Who in hell wants to dance by the light of the damned moon anyway?" Smith immediately changed the tune.

The outlaws grabbed each other and began dancing. After what seemed like a thousand years, but was only a few minutes, the outlaw leader put the gun away and grabbed his misses to dance. Smith played on, and on, and on, changing the tune when ordered.

The sweat rolled down his face and stung his eyes, his tongue lolled out, and his knees buckled under him, but he didn't dare stop. Someone shoved a bottle to his lips, and the nondrinker drank in the raw, strong whiskey.

The fiddler woke up three days later in a rooming house in Tombstone. Wright shook him awake and ordered him to get his fiddle and follow him. They went into a saloon, where after a meal at the outlaw's expense, Smith fiddled away the night.

Toles Cosper brought the first piano up on the Blue, in the northern part of Greenlee County. It was during the territorial days, and there weren't many pianos around. Cosper shipped it from Silver City, New Mexico and then burro packed, man packed, pushed, pulled, and maneuvered it out to his ranch. The fiddler gave the Cosper children lessons. Over the years he taught the grandchildren and great-grandchildren to play. He had more than fifty Cosper family pupils.

Not all of the fiddler's pupils came from fine, upstanding frontier families. One of his favorites, Joe Hale, was in and out of the penitentiary. Hale robbed the Duncan bank in 1909. He did a fourteen-year stretch for that. When he got out, he had some fame with Warner Brothers and with a Denver broadcasting station. He had every chance to make good with his talent, but seemed to prefer crime to music. A few years after his release, he robbed the Wilcox bank and landed back in prison.

Smith, the musician, seemed to draw trouble. Although he had not carried a gun since his youth, he found that sometimes his music landed him in life-threatening situations. Wandering down around the Mexican border, he lost his way and staggered, half-dead from hunger and thirst, into a camp of renegades. They fed him, then demanded he play. He played the harmonica, violin, guitar, and banjo; not satisfied, they made him dance to his own music.

When he was utterly exhausted, they dragged him to a stone wall. They had decided to shoot him for a spy. First the bandits poured tequila in him until he couldn't stand, then they demanded he play his own funeral dirge. He was so drunk by then he didn't care what they did to him. He wanted it over with as quickly as possible.

Out of sheer perversity, he began playing "La Paloma." The renegades stood there like statues, their eyes wide with surprise. He played the tune as a mockery to the crime they were about to commit. Twelve rifles aimed at his heart, but none of them fired. Then a whisper floated among them. The Mexicans' eyes never left Smith's face as they dropped their guns to their sides and formed two lines of six to a side.

A bedraggled, yet somehow imposing figure appeared at the head of the line. He strolled toward Smith and stopped short, staring at the fiddler. It was Poncho Villa. The sight of the general sobered Smith quicker than a cold dunking could. He thought he was in the throes of a bad hallucination. Was he already dead and in hell?

Slowly, evenly he changed the tune, sliding into "Celeta Linda." The killers crossed themselves, whispering, "Santa Maria." The fiddler played on and on until oblivion overcame him.

When John Smith woke up later, he never knew if it was days or weeks from his Mexican bandit ordeal. He found himself in a clean, comfortable bed in the Casa de Poncho Villa somewhere in the heart of the Durango Mountains. When he recovered, he began giving piano lessons to the general's pretty wife. The young woman had considerable natural talent and easily played the most difficult pieces. She was not the only talent in the family. Villa was possessed of a powerful voice akin to Caruso.

Smith stayed in the casa for six months, alone with the family when the bandit was away with his troops. When Villa was home, the musician gave him guitar lessons. Poncho Villa could not read, but he had an amazing ear for music. When the fiddler left, Villa paid him handsomely for the music lessons, gave him new clothes and shoes, and had him escorted across the border. Although invited back, he never returned.

For eighty-four years, the musician walked around the country spreading his musical cheer. His arches did not break down, he never had a corn, and he changed his socks and washed his feet when the notion struck him . . . usually in the spring, whether they needed it or not.

When he arrived in Duncan, he stayed for two years, the longest he had been in any one place. He didn't know how long he would be there; he was never sure when the mood would come upon him and he would start walking again.

Index of Names

Bibliography

Cleere, Jan, *Outlaw Tales of Arizona*, Guilford, CT: Two Dot, 2000.

Eppinga, Jane, *Arizona Sheriffs: Badges and Bad Men*, Tucson, AZ: Nuevo Publishers, 2006.

Federal Writers' Project, *Arizona: The Grand Canyon State*, revised by Joseph Miller, edited by Henry G. Alsberg and Harry Hansen, New York: Hasting House, 1966.

Lacy, Ann and Anne Valley-Fox, *Cowboys, Ranching and Cattle Trails: A New Mexico Federal Writers' Project Book*, Sante Fe, NM: Sunstone Press, 2013.

Lacy, Ann and Anne Valley-Fox, *Outlaws and Desperados: A New Mexico Federal Writers' Project Book*, Sante Fe, NM: Sunstone Press, 2008.

Mangione, Jerre, *The Dream and the Deal: The Federal Writers' Project, 1935–1942*, Pennsylvania: University of Pennsylvania Press, 1983.

Marriott, Barbara, *In Our Own Words: The Lives of Arizona Pioneer Women*, Tucson, AZ: Fireship Press, 2009.

Montana WPA, *Ornery Bunch: Tales and Anecdotes Collected by the Montana WPA*, Guilford, CT: Two Dot, 1999.

Sheridan, Thomas E., *Arizona: A History*, Tucson, AZ: University of Arizona Press, 1995.

Taylor, David, *Soul of a People: The WPA Writers' Project Uncovers Depression America*, Hoboken, NJ: John Wiley and Sons, Inc., 2009.

Turner, Jim, *Arizona: A Celebration of the Grand Canyon State*, Layton, UT: Gibbs Smith, 2011.

Wilson, R. Michael, *Great Train Robberies of the Old West*, Guilford, CT: Globe Pequot, 2006.

About the Author

An insatiable curiosity has led Barbara Marriott down the rabbit hole to some great adventures in the wonderland of book writing. In her checkerboard life, she has done such things as flown with the Blue Angels, created and edited a newspaper on the French Riviera, been a *Vogue* magazine Prix de Paris finalist, earned a Ph.D. in cultural anthropology, been a management consultant and trainer, been a college professor, and been listed in *Who's Who of American Women*.

Moving to Arizona eighteen years ago, Marriott turned her wild inquiring mind to the fascinating history of New Mexico and Arizona. She has written eight nonfiction historical books on the Southwest including *In Our Own Words: The Lives of Arizona Pioneer Women*, *Outlaw Tales of New Mexico*, and *Myths and Mysteries of New Mexico*; two works of historical fiction; and two historical nonfiction military books. Her reasoning for this eclectic mix: "I get bored easily." She lives in Tucson, Arizona.